Romeo and Julie

Gary Owen

T0228717

methuen | drama

LONDON • NEW YORK • OXFORD • NEW DELHI • SYDNEY

METHUEN DRAMA
Bloomsbury Publishing Plc
50 Bedford Square, London, WC1B 3DP, UK
1385 Broadway, New York, NY 10018, USA
29 Earlsfort Terrace, Dublin 2, Ireland

BLOOMSBURY, METHUEN DRAMA and the Methuen
Drama logo are trademarks of Bloomsbury Publishing Plc

First published in Great Britain by Methuen Drama 2023

Cover design by Jade Barnett Photography (Callum Scott Howells and Rosie
Sheehy) by Matt Hind. Art direction by National Theatre Graphic Design Studio

A catalogue record for this book is available from the British Library.

A catalog record for this book is available from the Library of Congress.

ISBN: PB: 978-1-3504-0894-4
ePDF: 978-1-3504-0896-8
eBook: 978-1-3504-0895-1

Series: Modern Plays

Typeset by Mark Heslington Ltd, Scarborough, North Yorkshire

To find out more about our authors and books visit
www.bloomsbury.com and sign up for our newsletters.

Romeo and Julie

a new play by Gary Owen

Cast in alphabetical order

Barb	**Catrin Aaron**
Col	**Paul Brennen**
Romy	**Callum Scott Howells**
Kath	**Anita Reynolds**
Julie	**Rosie Sheehy**

Director	**Rachel O'Riordan**
Set and Costume Designer	**Hayley Grindle**
Lighting Designer	**Jack Knowles**
Sound Designer	**Gregory Clarke**
Casting	**Bryony Jarvis-Taylor**
Intimacy Coordinator	**Imogen Knight**
Dialect Coach	**Patricia Logue**
Company Voice Work	**Cathleen McCarron**
Staff Director	**Kwame Owusu**

For the National Theatre

Producer	**Fran Miller**
Production Manager	**Heather Doole**
Dramaturg	**Nina Steiger**
Stage Manager	**Ian Farmery**
Deputy Stage Manager	**Alice Barber**
Assistant Stage Manager	**Shakira Taylor-Knight**
Deputy Production Manager	**Zara Janmohamed**
Project Draughting	**Emma Morris**
Digital Art	**Daniel Radley-Bennett**
Costume Supervisor	**Kirsty Blades**
Wigs, Hair & Make-up Supervisor	**Leanne Lashbrook**
Running Wardrobe Supervisor	**Ruth Williams**
Prop Buyer	**Kinga Czynciel**
Prop Coordinator	**Michelle McLucas**
Puppetry	**Laura Cubitt**

Lighting Supervisors	**Jack Champion and Jack Williams**
Lighting Associate	**Aaron Porter**
Lighting Programmer	**Nadene Wheatley**
Production Sound Engineer	**Sarah Weltman**
Sound Operator	**Clio Nonis**
Stage Supervisors	**Lee Harrington and Dave Tuff**
Rigging Supervisor	**Riche Tarr**
Construction Supervisor	**Paul Sheppard**
Scenic Art Supervisor	**Alice Collie**
Production Photographer	**Marc Brenner**

For Sherman Theatre, Cardiff

Head of Production and Planning	**Mandy Ivory-Castile**
Technical Manager	**Rachel Mortimer**
Company Stage Manager	**Josh Miles**
Assistant Stage Manager	**Emily Howard**

Romeo and Julie is a National Theatre and Sherman Theatre co-production.

Opening

Dorfman Theatre, 21 February 2023

Sherman Theatre, Cardiff, 13 April 2023

Romeo and Julie

This play is dedicated to

Emily McLaughlin, for kicking it off

Nina Steiger, for bundling it over the line

And to Rachel O'Riordan,
For chewing up the hard yards with me,
As ever.

Characters

Romy
Julie
Barb
Kath
Col

Act One

Scene One

Barb's *flat. A combined living room and kitchen. A bed settee. A Moses basket. No sound from within it.*

On comes **Barb**.

She stops. Sniffs the air.

Walks over to the Moses basket. Looks down. She calls off.

Barb   Romy.

No answer.

Romy!

No answer.

ROMEO. ANTHONY. JONES.

She says it Row-mayo. As in Alfa.

On comes **Romy**.

Barb *nods come over here take a look at this.*

Romy *comes over.*

Looks down into the Moses basket.

Romy   Shit.

Barb   Correct. That is what me and your nan used to call, a gale force poo-nami.

Romy   How does something so tiny, have that / much shit in her –

Barb   That's not even the thing.

Romy   It looks like the thing.

Barb   The thing is – how does she do a shit like that, and sleep through it?

Romy   Seen you do worse.

Barb   Oi!

She gives him a light cuff. Not vicious, but not joking either.

Romy   Dunno where to start.

Barb   Anywhere you like, it's all gonna be shit.

She hands him a pack of wipes, as he reaches into the basket.

He's unpopping the poppers of **Niamh***'s babygro. Switches between a baby voice to talk to* **Niamh***, normal voice to* **Barb***.*

Romy   Nevey, what have you done? (*A discovery.*) It's from her ankles, to her wrists. How's it get to her wrists?

Barb   Cos of the force it comes out her arse.

Romy*'s peeled the babygro off* **Niamh***. Holds it in pinched thumb and finger.*

Romy   What do I do with this?

Barb   Leave it soak down the toilet a couple hours. I always did with yours.

Romy *offers it to her.*

Barb   I'm not touching it!

Romy *gives up. Heads off to the toilet.*

Barb   And don't you dare drip wet shit on my floor.

Romy   How'm I gonna stop it?

Barb   Well, catch it, dear Romy, with your bloody hand.

Romy *realises she's not joking.*

Romy   Oh my God . . .

He extends his other hand, catches the runny shit dripping from the sodden baby gro.

Gurgles from the basket.

Romy   I know darlin, back in two secs. (*Normal voice.*) Oh my God, I am gonna puke . . .

Barb   And don't you dare puke on my floor either.

Romy *heads off to the toilet.* **Barb** *goes back to the basket.*

Barb   Don't try those eyes on me, young lady. I am not bloody soft like your dad.

Romy *returns with a* Star Wars/Avengers *or similar bath sheet.*

Lays it on the mat.

Brings the Moses basket over to the mat.

Transfers the shitty baby.

Romy   There you go, my darlin. Just gonna get you all cleaned up now, is that alright?

He picks up a wet wipe.

Barb   Thank your stars she's still on the milk. Cos while they're on the milk, their shit doesn't really smell.

Romy   It smells from here.

Barb   Couple months now when she's on proper food, it's gonna be like actual human shit you're cleaning up. This stuff is like –

Romy   You are beautiful aren't you. All your little fat rolls.

With all the little bits of shit smeared under them oh my God . . .

Barb   . . . it's like you know you get like a fruit chutney with poppadoms from the Cottage? It's like that.

Romy *comes to a stop.*

Barb   What?

Romy   Chutney and poppadoms from the Cottage. That's my favourite bit.

Barb   Yeah, they do 'em in just that bit too much oil / I think it is

Romy   Except now when I have 'em, I'm gonna be / thinking about

Barb   Don't be so daft! (*To the baby.*) Your daddy's daft, isn't he. Cos when's he gonna be getting an Indian? *Never.* He can't afford it.

Romy's *reached the end of the wet wipes. Holds up the empty packet.*

Romy   Can you get me another pack of these?

Barb   From where?

Romy   This is the last one?

Barb   I dunno, is it?

Romy   What'm I gonna do, she's covered.

He's made a pile of dirty wet wipes by the changing mat.

Barb   Half those you've hardly used.

He starts picking through the used wipes, picks up the least soiled.

Romy   It's all in her –

Barb   What?

Romy   The folds of her . . . lady bits.

Barb   And?

Romy   It feels a bit . . . weird. Going in there.

Barb   She's your *daughter.*

Romy   Feels like it might a bit wrong.

Barb   Fair enough then just leave your baby daughter with a shitty vagina, why not –

Romy   Alright, alright, bloody hell –

He gets to wiping.

It strikes **Barb** *what she's going to say next.*

Barb   You think I didn't have to clear your bits out often enough.

Romy *ignores her, keeps working.*

Barb   You think cleaning a shitty fanny's hard work, you try getting it out from under a foreskin.

Romy   OH. MY. GOD.

Barb (*all innocence*)   What?

He gets back to cleaning.

Barb *watches him work.*

Romy (*to the baby*)   Nearly finished. Nearly done.

He's finished cleaning her. Gets the bum cream.

Smears it on.

Romy   She's conked out again.

Barb   She haven't?

Romy   Look!

Barb   'S only having to do a shit woke her up, she's shattered love her.

Romy *starts getting a fresh nappy and babygro on* **Niamh.**

Barb   Gonna have a job cleaning out that Moses basket.

Romy   Yup.

He picks up the nappy pack to get a fresh nappy; it's obviously the last one in the pack. He puts down the empty plastic wrapper.

Barb *sees this; but doesn't comment.*

Romy *doesn't know what to do for a second.*

Then just gets the nappy on **Niamh.**

Barb   How many nappies you got for the night, Ro?

Romy *busies himself taking apart the Moses basket.*

Barb   How many d'you say?

Romy   One.

Barb   Is that one nappy spare . . . or one nappy, as in the one that's on her now.

Romy *stops what he's doing.*

Barb   Cos there is no way she's getting through the night on one nappy.

Romy   I know.

Barb   What're you gonna do then?

He doesn't answer.

Barb   Ro?

He doesn't answer.

Then he moves.

Barb   Romy?

He goes out, not to the bedroom.

Comes back.

He's carrying a yellow hygiene waste bag.

Romy   There was a couple I took off her yesterday I shouldn't've, barely a drop in them.

Barb   You're gonna put shitty nappies back on her?

Romy   No! No, that's what I'm saying, they were just a bit wet, I was stupid taking them off her . . .

He unties the bag. The smell from within – a few days of sodden nappies – is vile.

Romy   Oh Jesus that stinks . . .

Barb   In you dive then.

He hesitates.

Barb   Go on!

Romy   Or . . . you lend me a coupla quid, I run out to Tesco's –

Barb   Tesco's is shut –

Romy   Big Tesco's, I'll run, and –

Barb   No.

Romy   Mum.

Barb   I told you, Romy. I brought my kids up already. I am not doing it again.

Romy   This *one* time.

Barb   But it won't be.

Romy   Right then.

He turns away.

Starts going through the nappies in the hygiene bag, sniffing them to see if they are shitty or just pissy.

Sniffs a few.

And stops.

Romy   Mum.

She looks at him.

Romy   I can't.

She knows what he's saying.

Romy   I can't any more.

Barb *gets up straight away.*

Goes to him.

Romy   I can't.

She hugs him; he hugs her back.

Romy   She wakes me up and soon as I wake all I can think is when I can go back to sleep and I am so tired all the time I think I'm gonna puke from it and I never even knew you could be so tired you'd wanna puke –

Barb   This is what I been saying –

Romy   – and I'm getting angry with her. I get angry with her for waking. And angry with her for wetting her nappy cos I can't afford more nappies. And angry with her for shitting cos I can't afford more wipes. And this –

Barb   What've I been telling you?

Romy   – this is the bit I thought I could do!

Barb   Look. Look.

I have been a crap mum to all of you and I know it but I think I must've done some of it right. I must've, the way you've gone at it tryna be a dad to her.

Romy   I am her dad.

Barb   I know, I know.

But you're also a kid. You're a kid yourself.

And what I been saying to you all along is, it's too much for you.

Isn't it.

He doesn't answer.

Barb   Isn't it?

He doesn't answer.

Barb   Sweetheart?

Romy   It is yeah.

Barb   That's so brave. That's so brave of you saying that.

She wipes his eyes.

Barb   I have been *so* proud of you.

But shall we stop this now?

For her good, as well as yours.

Romy   For her?

Barb   Yes!

Romy   It's best, for her?

Barb   Course!

Romy   She's this tiny little thing. But she's too much.

Barb   Alright then. Brave boy. My brave, brave boy.

She goes to her purse. Gets out a twenty.

Gives it to him.

Romy   What's this?

Barb   Head into town, have a few drinks, crash wherever.
I'll phone the social tomorrow. I'll pack her stuff. I'll take
her in. She'll be with a foster family by tea time. And you can
come home. And she'll be gone. And we'll have a big cry.
And next week, you start again. Not being a dad anymore.
Just being a kid.

Romy   You'll do all that for me?

Barb   Course.

He hugs her. She strokes his hair. They part.

Barb   Go on, get there before last orders.

Romy   There is no last orders any more. Everywhere just
stays open.

He heads to pick up a coat, heads for the door.

Stops.

Romy   I'll just go and say goodbye.

Barb   I wouldn't.

Romy   I'll just go and see her.

Barb   She's asleep, let her be.

Romy   I'm not gonna wake her, I'm just gonna look.

Barb   Best not.

He goes to walk past her.

She puts her arm out, sort of tries to stop him.

Romy   Mum!

Barb   You do not go in there. I am telling you now, don't you do it.

He – not roughly, but firmly – pushes her arm aside.

Barb   Romy!

He heads on, ignoring her. Goes into the bedroom. **Barb** *waits.*

Paces.

Drinks.

Romy *returns.*

Niamh, *wrapped in a blanket, on his shoulder.*

Barb   Oh Jesus . . .

Romy *looks at her.*

Barb   I bloody knew it.

Romy   She just – wriggled, and woke, and looked at me –

Barb   Why can't you just *listen* –

Romy   And I picked her up. And she flopped down on me. Snuffling in my neck. And I went to put her down –

– and I couldn't.

I was thinking – this little girl. This is the last time she's gonna be hugged by her daddy, in her whole, whole life. And she's got no idea. She's just –

Barb   I know.

Romy   I just couldn't.

Barb   I know. I know you couldn't.

You stupid, stupid, stupid bloody *coward*.

Scene Two

The STAR hub in Tremorfa. The cafe area, in front of the pool.

Romy *slumped not quite asleep at one of the tables. He's sitting with his back to one of the windows onto the pool. A bag with baby kit on the table in front of him.*

Niamh *asleep in a buggy nearby but not right next to him.*

Julie *approaches. She's got a couple of bags – a rucksack and a little jute shopping bag – and her arms full of books and folders.*

Julie *waits near the table, expecting* **Romy** *to look up. He doesn't. She clears her throat.*

No response.

Clears her throat a bit more emphatically.

No response.

Julie   Hello?

No response.

Julie   Are you alive?

No response.

She rearranges herself so she can – just about – hold all her folders and the like with one hand, and reaches out with her free hand to prod him.

Romy *immediately sits bolt upright.*

Romy   Yeah I'm coming now!

Julie   Bloody hell!

He stares at her.

Romy   What're you looking at me like that for?

Julie   I jabbed you and you jumped / and

Romy   What're you jabbing me for?

Julie   See if you were dead.

Romy   Nearly had a bloody heart attack thanks to you so, maybe . . .

Julie   I think if you actually had a heart attack you'd be rolling round on the floor instead of staring at me with that drippy look on your face.

Romy *alters the look on his face. Not as a joke, just not wanting to look drippy.*

Julie   Do you need all this table? Cos I know this is strictly the cafe area not the library study area? But I got loads to do and in the study area there's a gang of ten-year-olds building an escape the sex dungeon obby on Roblox whatever the hell that is and they're just very very very loud.

Romy   Right.

Julie *begins putting her stuff down. A bag on a chair, a bag on the floor. Folders on the table. She gets books from a bag, and a laptop. Starts opening up and spreading out folders. She's taking up so much space that her stuff is pushing in front of where **Romy** is sitting.*

Julie   If you're not actually using the table does that bag actually need to be on it? Or could it go on the floor?

Romy   Christ, sorry, Karen.

Julie   What did you say to me?

Romy   Nothing.

He moves the bag.

Julie   Thank you.

He shifts down the bench far enough that he's not really sitting at the table any more. **Julie**'s *gets to work, pulls up a document on her laptop. Then sort of stops.*

Julie   So, how long've you been homeless?

Romy   Sorry, what?

Julie   There's an app I got on my phone? I tell them where I saw you and they get you . . . services.

For the homeless.

Romy   I live on Ordell Street.

Julie   Oh, just with you sleeping in here, I thought – and you look a bit –

Romy   Homeless.

Julie   And you do smell a bit of sick.

Romy   I probably do. Not my sick though.

Julie   Oh, well, fair enough then.

Romy   I was just really tired so I / flopped down –

Julie   My dad's like that, can sleep anywhere.

Romy   I'm on the bed-settee at my mum's, it's not the comfiest. And my mum's a bit –

He's not sure how to put it.

Julie   Bit of a handful? Tell me about it. Have you done this, have you done that, on and / bloody on –

Romy (*over her*)   Bit of a massive alcoholic.

Julie   Oh.

Romy   Yeah, it's a pain.

Julie   My mum she's just . . . a bit much every now and again.

Romy   Lucky you.

Julie   Yeah, totally.

A little awkward pause.

So I've got to – [get on with my work].

Romy   You crack on.

Julie *gets into her work.*

Romy *watches her.*

Julie   Sorry, could you not watch me?

Romy   Yeah, sorry.

He makes a point of turning away.

Julie *gets back to her physics.*

Romy *drinks from a bottle of water.*

Julie *looks up at the sound of him drinking.*

So he stops drinking.

She looks back to her computer.

Tries to get to work.

Fiddles with the touchpad.

Stabs at the screen.

Julie   Updates. Of course.

She watches the computer chug away for a bit. Then –

Julie   So where d'you live, with your alcoholic mum?

Romy   . . . Ordell Street?

Julie   I'm Moorland Road.

Romy   Just moved?

Julie   Uh . . . *no.*

Romy   How come I don't know you from school?

Julie   I go to Bro Edern.

Romy   The Welsh school?

Julie   They're all Welsh schools.

Romy   Welsh-language one.

Julie   Yeah.

Romy   Posh then.

Julie   I am not posh cos I go to a Welsh school . . .

Romy   You know you are.

Nearly a smile from her.

Julie   Well, compared to you . . .

Romy   So what're you studying?

She holds up a book.

Romy   Left my glasses home.

Julie   Physics.

Romy   Love that. Love physics.

Julie   Oh yeah? Which bits of it?

Romy   D'you know what? I've never done any physics I didn't love.

Julie   I bet you haven't . . .

Romy   What bit are you doing?

Julie   Relativistic momentum.

Romy   Yeah. Classic.

Julie   That's funny you say that, that it's classic. And you will never know why.

Romy   You explain it to me then.

Julie   I have actually got stuff to be getting on with.

Romy   No, fair play.

Julie *gets on.*

Romy   Why you doing that then? Relativistic momentum.

He's not going to stop.

Julie   Ultimately, so I can work on the theory of everything.

Romy   A what now?

Julie   The theory of everything.

Romy   The theory of what I'm gonna have for breakfast tomorrow morning?

Julie   No.

Romy   Breakfast's part of everything.

Julie   When in physics we say a theory of everything, we mean a theory that attempts to reconcile the theory of relativity with quantum theory.

Romy   The fuck's that?

Julie   Do you actually want to know?

Romy   Never before in my life no but actually now yeah.

Julie   Okay. There are two important theories in modern physics. The theory of relativity handles all the big, massive things – stars, galaxies. And then quantum theory deals with all the really tiny things – everything smaller than an atom. And both theories work really well. But they don't work together. They don't match up in the middle.

Romy   Keeps you up at night does it, worrying about that?

Julie   Some things are tiny and massive at the same time?

Romy   Yeah, they are.

This means something for **Romy**, *and* **Julie** *can see it means something: but she can't tell what.*

Julie   Like, the start of the universe, at the Big Bang, everything was packed into one point. So it was tiny, because it was one point. And massive, cos it contained all the universe. We need a theory that can handle tiny things, and massive things. And we call that the theory of everything. And till we've got it, we'll never understand where the universe came from.

He looks at her.

Romy   You're trying to work out where the universe came from, sat in the caff, in the STAR . . . in Tremorfa?

Julie   When I was twelve my dad took me up the mountains. And you could see stars, everywhere, and this band of silver across the night which is the Milky Way, the rest of our galaxy. And I said to my dad, where's it all come from? My dad says, I dunno. And go, right. I'm gonna find out then.

Romy   You were a fuckin weird twelve-year-old.

Julie   All the other twelve-year-olds thought so.

Julie   And Mum said there's this bionic bloke called Stephen Hawking at Cambridge University, he's working on a theory of everything to figure out where everything comes from. And I said, right. I'll go there and help him with that.

Romy   Isn't he dead? Stephen Hawking.

Julie   That'll be why he's not answering my texts.

He's looking at her.

Romy   I've never met anybody who says stuff like that.

Julie   Like what?

Romy   Like – I'm going to Cambridge University. Like you just can.

Like that's a thing that can happen in your life.

Something in the way he's looking at her now is making her suddenly self-conscious.

Julie   Well, you can't *just* do it. You have to absolutely smash the fuck out of your A levels.

Romy   And you're gonna, aren't you.

Julie   Not if I carry on like this, chatting to you.

She starts to focus on her work again.

Romy   Nobody's making you chat to me. It just seems like you want to.

Chat to me.

She ignores him.

Romy   Whole cafe to sit in but you had to share my table.

Julie   Just don't. Just don't do it.

Romy   What?

Julie   The getting flirty thing.

Romy   I didn't start it, love.

She's working.

Romy   Besides if I was getting flirty, you wouldn't know about it.

She carries on working. She heard the mistake but she's going to let it go. She can't let it go.

Julie   Sorry, no, you've got that wrong. It's, 'If I was getting flirty, you'd know about it.' Cause the power of your flirting would be so irresistible I'd find / myself bending –

Romy   Nah.

Julie   'Nah'?

Romy   If I was getting flirty, you *wouldn't* know about it.

Because you wouldn't even realise it was happening.

You'd just be having a really nice time chatting to me.

And then you'd find yourself tapping your number into my phone because . . . why would you not?

They're looking at each other.

Niamh *makes a tiny noise. The tiniest possible noise. But it's the excuse* **Julie** *needs.*

Julie   And now that sodding baby's waking up.

Romy *watches* **Niamh**, *doesn't move to her. Then –*

Romy   Nah, we got another five minutes yet.

Julie *doesn't follow – how can he know?*

Romy   She's mine.

Julie   Who is?

Romy   The baby.

Julie   You babysitting?

Romy   I don't think you can babysit your own daughter.

Julie   *Oh.*

Romy   And I know she's not gonna wake yet because that little sniffle she did? That's the noise she makes when she does a poo in her sleep. And she'll sleep through that happily enough cos it's all nice and warm in her nappy. But then in five minutes when it gets all cold and clammy, she is not gonna like that.

Don't worry I'll take her off before she starts screaming.

Julie   How old are you?

Romy   Eighteen.

Julie   I could never do that. I haven't got a maternal bone in my body.

Romy   Me neither.

Julie   And . . . you're not in school?

Romy *shakes his head.*

Julie   What d'you do then?

Romy   When do you think a baby switches off?

Julie   Don't you get bored?

Romy   All the time. But it's just me looking after her so . . .

Julie   Her mum's not –

Romy   Not fucking interested no.

And after a bit you're too tired to be bored so you're just, you know, grabbing naps wherever you can. Like in the caff at the STAR. Hoping nobody comes along and wakes you up.

Julie   But don't you feel like . . .

'Feel like giving up and running away?' But she can't say that.

Julie   . . . you know.

Romy   Every single day.

But there's no one else. And she needs me.

So I'm hers. Till she doesn't need me anymore.

He's too exposed. He breaks the moment between them.

Anyway I best be moving before she really kicks off . . .

He gets up. He's going. He's really going.

Julie   It's just: one of the million things I've got to do for my uni application is, at school we have this Community Challenge? Which is a challenge, to help the community? So what if I help you?

Romy   Help me how?

Julie   Like – I could look after your baby for you? For a bit.

Romy   You know anything about babies?

Julie   I used to be one.

Romy   And babysitting for me counts as helping the community?

Julie   Single dad with an alcoholic mum? You're so community. It doesn't get more community than you.

Romy   And you think you'd help me, do you? Not just be another thing I gotta stress about?

He's genuinely defensive, closed to her. She has to snap him out of it.

Julie   How hard could it be – compared to relativistic momentum.

Romy's *blank – and then smiles.*

Julie   What?

Romy   You haven't got a clue. You are literally clue-less. I can tell by the big smug grin.

Julie   Wipe it off my face, then.

He extends a hand.

Romy   I'm Romy, by the way.

Julie   Hiya, I'm Julie.

Romy   Nice to meet you, Julie. So I'll give you a ring shall I, set up when you can come round and help me out?

Julie   Yeah sure.

Romy   Okay then.

His demeanour shifts. He hands her his phone.

Romy   Be a love – tap your number into that.

Scene Three

Barb's *flat. Tidier than when we saw it last.* **Romy** *rushing around putting things away.*

Julie *arrives.* **Romy** *goes to get her.*

They enter.

Romy   So this is my mum's.

Shithole isn't it.

Julie   I've seen worse. On shows about hoarders, that kind of thing.

Where's Niamh?

Romy   She's gone down. That's what you say when babies go to / sleep.

Julie   Yeah I'm not an idiot.

Romy   She's in my mum's room.

Julie's *getting something out of her bag.*

Julie   I've got this form you've got to fill out to say you're happy with – me, really.

Romy   I don't know I am yet.

He gets rid of the form.

Julie   Well, great, cos I get better marks if you say I was rubbish to start but I kept at it and really tried not to be? Shows resilience. Apparently that's number one attribute young people need to face the future. Not ambition or having big dreams – just being able to take a kicking.

She takes off her fleece.

Romy   You off down the gym after?

Julie   Been.

Romy   Was gonna say, you smell a bit sweaty.

She gives him the finger.

Romy   Well, today I been to rhyme time at the library, few laps round the park, Lidl; then soft play in Pen-y-lan leisure centre.

Julie   Busy day.

Romy   Can't miss soft play at Pen-y-lan, it's the best one, any under-five'll tell you that. Plus that's where all the yummiest mummies go, so you know: I don't mind it myself.

Julie   You wanna . . . go for a walk?

Romy   What if she wakes up while I'm out?

Julie   And what would you do, if she woke up?

Romy   Feed her.

Julie   Then that's what I'll do.

Romy   Do you know how to make formula?

Julie   Has it got instructions on it?

Romy   Yeah.

Julie   Then I'll just read / them and –

Romy   Right I know – we'll practise.

He picks up her bag.

Got anything valuable in here?

Julie   Gym kit

He shifts how he's carrying it, so he's cradling it in his arm.

Romy   So now it's your baby.

Julie   Weird-looking baby.

Romy   Ugly as fuck, at least mine's gorgeous.

Julie   I have not got a fucking ugly / baby –

Romy Right and she's waking up now. She's starting to cry. What you gonna do?

Julie Feed her.

Romy Go on then.

Julie I don't know how / to –

Romy Cos I'm nice I made up some formula for you? By there.

Julie *finds the formula.*

Julie Right so how do I do it?

Romy You're just gonna give it to her?

Julie You said she wanted a / feed –

Romy Right temperature is it?

Julie What temperature do babies like it?

Romy The temperature it would be if it came out your boob.

Julie Okay.

She sticks the bottle down, or up, her top.

Romy What are you doing?

Julie You said it had to be the same temperature as if it was coming out of my boobs –

She stops.

Julie Okay so any part of my body will do.

Romy People use the inside of their arm, a lot?

Julie *tests the bottle against the inside of her forearm.*

Romy What d'you think?

Julie No idea.

Romy You are absolutely fuckin smashing this.

Julie   You're such an amazing teacher, how could / I not?

Romy   She is seconds from total meltdown now so you best give it to her then.

He offers **Julie** *her bag, holding it as if it were a baby.*

Julie *manages to take the bag while not dropping the bottle.*

Romy   Right so her head's just flopped back cos you weren't supporting it and she's maybe broken her neck –

Julie *shifts her grip.*

Julie   Now what do I just stick it in?

Romy   You offer it up to her lips. And you let her go for it.

Julie   Like this?

Romy   No!

Julie   What's wrong with this?

Romy   See how you're holding it straight up? That's too fast. She'll get too much air with the milk and then she'll have trapped wind and that's gonna be bad for everyone.

Julie   So what then?

Romy   Keep the bottle just a bit above level. And give her little breaks. If she seems like she's turning away from the bottle, don't chase it back into her mouth. Let her show you what she wants.

Julie*'s really trying – to let a bag show her what it wants.* **Romy** *can't help but smile at her concentration.*

Julie   Oh you are loving this.

Romy   I'd wipe the formula off your bag though, bloody stinks when it goes off.

Julie *stops the mime. Shifts so she's holding the bag at her side, and the bottle in her other hand.* **Romy** *takes the bottle off her, puts it somewhere.*

Romy   So what else do you need to know?

Julie   You and . . . Niamh's mum you're not . . .

Romy   I meant about looking after babies.

Julie   You see her much?

Romy   Not at all no.

It was just a one-night thing – well, one night and then again the morning after cos why / not –

Julie   Didn't need to hear that . . .

Romy   – and I thought, nice one, see you round.

But then bit after she said she was pregnant and I was . . . oh fuck. But she said don't worry I'm gonna get a –

Julie   Abortion.

Romy   Which was like massive relief for me –

Julie   Well, obviously.

Romy   But then she changed her mind.

She decided she wanted to have it.

So I said fair enough, if that's what you want. You are the woman after all.

But then once she had the baby – it was all too much. She wanted to give Niamh up for adoption.

I couldn't stop thinking – this little girl. The first thing that happens in her life is everyone turning their back on her.

And then it sort of just hit me one day – that I was her dad. Or actually I wasn't. I was some bloke who fucked her mum and got her up the duff.

But I could be her dad.

So I said to Niamh's mum, I'll take her. You don't have to do anything. You give her to me, and walk away.

If you can.

Julie   Bloody hell.

Romy   And then I talked to my mum about it and she said Christ sake Romy don't be a twat, absolutely no bloody way can you take on a baby, you haven't got a clue, you haven't got the balls –

Julie   Your *mum* said that to you?

Romy   She's a treat when she's sober.

And I thought, well, my mum has brought up kids so she knows what it's actually like.

And she knows me better than anyone so she knows what I'm actually like.

So if she thinks I'm not up to raising a baby then she's probably right.

But by then I'd already said I'd have Niamh.

And I didn't really know how I could get out of it.

Anyway.

I mean if you want you can just catch up on your physics or whatever, while Nevey's still asleep.

Julie   Yeah, sure.

She doesn't get to work.

You know my mum's not really my mum.

I mean she a hundred per cent is, I hate saying she's not. But my biological mum, she died when I was little.

Romy   I'm so sorry.

Julie   Yeah. Thanks.

I mean I was tiny.

Romy   Still, losing your mum –

Julie   Like I was two. I don't remember her. So it's almost like I didn't lose her. And I always feel awful saying that cos – like my dad lost her.

Romy   And she lost you.

Julie   Yeah.

Romy   And you lost her too.

Julie   But it's like it never happened, cos I can't remember / it –

Romy   Yeah it did.

A little moment before **Julie** *decides not to respond.*

Julie   And my dad had to cope with me on his own, and grieving and everything – until Kath came along.

Romy   And she took you on.

Julie   And now she bollocks me all day and makes my life miserable.

And I suppose that makes her my mum.

A moment. They look at each other. And then look away.

Julie   I don't think I'm in the mood to work now.

Romy   No.

Watch a film or something?

Julie   What you got?

Romy   Well, last week my mum passed the cancer shop and they were doing lucky dip ten DVDs for a pound. And it was my birthday. So guess what I got?

Julie   Ten DVDs?

He's looking for something.

Romy   And only three of them were exercise videos.

Julie   Bit of wank material at least. (*Beat.*) You bloody have as well!

Romy   You take what you can get when you can't afford Netflix.

Julie   I mean I've got Netflix on my phone, so . . . seen *Stranger Things*?

Romy   Obviously not.

Julie   Well, then . . .

She gets out her phone.

Romy   So how we gonna like / do this?

Julie   Well we'll have to sit [together] – like cos my phone's really small –

Romy   Yeah, no –

Julie   Is that alright?

Romy   Yeah, no worries.

They sit together. A little bit of rearranging of stuff to accommodate this and find a way to prop the phone up on something.

Julie *sits down.*

And then **Romy** *sits down near her. But not next to her.*

Romy   You alright?

Julie   Yeah good.

She starts the episode.

Julie   Can you see?

Romy   Yeah fine.

Julie   Yeah?

She sort of leans over so she's seeing the phone from where **Romy** *is sitting.*

Julie   Cos I can't see bugger all from there. Do I actually smell?

Romy   No!

Julie   I did shower after the gym.

Romy   Yeah, you smell of, like, shower gel, it's really nice.

Julie   What I smell of is not bloody shower gel, mate.

Romy   I'm just saying it's nice.

Julie   So do you wanna just . . . budge up a bit?

He looks at her.

Romy   Yeah okay.

He budges up.

Julie   Alright?

Romy   Yep.

And she budges up a bit too.

They're now sitting right next to each other, so their bodies are touching.

And they're very aware of how their bodies are touching.

Romy's *keeping his eyes very much fixed on the screen.*

Julie's *maybe glancing at him.*

His hands in his lap.

Julie   Jesus, what's up with your hands?

He snatches his hand away, hides it.

Romy   It's just dry skin it is.

Julie   Let me see.

Romy   Cos I have to wash my hands loads. Cos of all the nappy changes. And then we haven't got a washing machine, so I have to do all Nevey's stuff in the bath.

Julie   It's cracked through to blood and everything. Does it hurt?

Romy   Only when I have to wash my hands. Or use them.

Julie   I know what'll sort that.

She goes in her bag. Gets out a little tub.

Romy   Looks like fat off burgers.

Julie   Coconut oil is solid at room temperature, yes. Rub it in your hands.

Romy   How? It's a lump.

Julie   Don't be so useless.

She scoops up a chunk of the solid oil.

Rubs it between her fingers.

Julie   Give us your hand.

Takes one of his hands. Examines it.

Julie   This'll sort out the dry skin, and as well as that it is a bit antiseptic?

Romy   Alright, yeah.

Julie   So that does mean –

She rubs it in his palm. He yelps.

Julie   – that it will slightly sting where the skin's broken.

Romy   Slightly?

Julie   You wuss.

She keeps going, turning his hand over, rubbing the oil into the palm and the back of his hand.

She's very gentle, and very thorough

*It's the first time **Romy** has been touched by an adult in a way that is intimate and affectionate and kind in a very long time.*

And it has an the entirely predictable effect on him. He shifts how he sits.

Julie *senses his sudden and specific uncomfortableness.*

She knows what's going on. And she doesn't hate it.

Julie   You alright?

Romy   Yeah I'm good.

Julie   Stops stinging after a sec though doesn't it.

Romy   Mm.

Julie   Other hand then.

He offers his other hand.

And maybe not such a baby about it this time?

They don't speak as she works.

She's deliberately taking longer over it this time.

It's a bit more sensual than therapeutic.

He watches her face, as she looks at his hand.

She senses his gaze; looks up.

They're looking at each other, as she holds his hand in both hers.

Just looking at each other.

And then **Julie** *just ever so slightly tilts her head a tiny bit.*

And he does . . . ever so slightly tilts his.

And she every so slightly moves her head nearer his.

They're about to kiss, when –

– she pulls back.

Julie   Alright we can do this but you have to absolutely promise not to fall in love with me. I am off in a few months and I don't wanna break your heart.

I mean I slightly do but that's a really bad part of me and I'm fighting it down.

Romy   I'm not gonna fall in love with you.

Julie   Just with boys because I'm like much much cleverer than them and I don't do that much to hide it they either find it obnoxious or they fall for it. And you / are absolutely –

Romy   I'm actually finding you a bit annoying.

She's closing on him again.

Julie   Yeah you're annoyed how much you're falling for me.

They're going to kiss –

– and then he pulls back.

Romy   And you have to promise not to fall in love with me.

Julie   There is no way I'm gonna fall in love with you.

Romy   No?

Julie   Absolutely no chance / at all –

He kisses her. Breaks it.

She's staring at him.

Romy   You were saying?

She grabs his face, starts snogging him.

– and his phone goes. It's a really specific tone, like an alarm. He breaks off.

Julie   Are you actually getting that?

Romy   It's my mum.

(*As he talks* **Romy** *is struggling to subtly do what men do to subdue an inconvenient erection: he reaches down into his pants, pushes his penis back so it's against his lower belly, then uses the waistband of his pants and trackie bottoms to hold it down, then pulls his t-shirt down as far as it will go.*)

Julie *watching him throughout.*

Romy (*on phone*)   Yeah what.

Mum?

Julie   Do you realise what was about to happen then?

Romy (*on phone*)   Any idea at all?

Could you ask someone?

Okay where to in Ely?

Call apparently cuts.

Julie   What's up?

Romy   My mum is up. Up in fucking Ely.

Romy's *phone goes again.*

Romy (*on phone*)   I know you are.

Cos we just talked like thirty seconds ago.

And you were telling me you –

– no I am here.

I have answered.

This is me now talking to [you] –

The call cuts.

Romy   She was meeting some old friend at the Gatekeeper and now she's gone back to someone's house somewhere in Ely but she doesn't know where.

Julie   Is she gonna be alright?

Romy   She starts drinking tea time that's it, she's gone.

Phone goes again.

Well, what number? Well, that doesn't really help me [does it] –

The call cuts again.

Romy   She's locked herself in the toilet cos there are people after her.

Julie   What're you gonna do?

*Looking at **Julie**: he decides.*

Romy   Go and get her.

*He starts getting things together to take **Niamh** out. He's quick, knows what he's doing.*

Julie   How're you getting there?

Romy   Well, I'm broke so I'm gonna have to walk aren't I.

Julie   That's gonna take hours –

Romy   Oh I know. I'm gonna have to stick Niamh in her pram and walk her hours across town in the cold and the rain to some fuckin party in Ely cos my fuckin / mum –

Julie   Can't somebody else have her?

Romy   There isn't anybody else, there's just me.

He's moving, getting stuff together.

Julie   There's not just you.

Romy   And then I'm gonna have to drag Mum back across town / when she's pissed and –

Julie   There's not just you. There's me.

Romy   You?

Julie   I could have her. She'll probably just sleep.

Romy   I promise you, she will not.

Julie   Then I'll – feed her? I have practised.

Romy   And when she needs her nappy changed?

Julie   Take old nappy off, put new nappy on.

Romy   You have to clean all the shit off her before you put the new nappy on.

Julie   Obviously. I thought that was too obvious to say.

Romy   You have to get it out of all her – nooks and crannies.

Julie   Out of her –

Romy   Like all the rolls of fat on her thighs and . . . her vagina.

Julie   I'll be fine dealing with her vagina. I've been dealing with my own for years. Now go and get your mum.

He doesn't know what to say.

Romy   You said yourself you haven't got a maternal bone in you.

Julie   That's two of us then.

He decides.

Romy   I'm gonna go, I'm gonna get my mum, and I'm gonna fuckin kill her.

Julie   I'll mind Niamh while you bury the body.

He walks up to **Julie**, *no hesitation, takes her face in his hands and kisses her. There's nothing nervy or sleazy about it. Just heartfelt gratitude.*

Romy   Thank you.

Julie   . . . any time.

Romy *grabs a hoodie and heads off.*

Romy   And don't forget she needs winding after every feed.

Julie   Yeah obviously.

Once he's gone, **Julie** *picks up her phone.*

Julie   Siri – what is winding?

Scene Four

Col *and* **Kath**'s *place. Kitchen.* **Julie**'s *laptop on the table.*

Kath   You should know her password.

Col   It isn't passwords any more.

Kath   What is it then?

Col   Fingerprints.

Kath   You should have a copy of her fingerprint on I don't know plastic film or something.

If computers was one of my things, I'd have a copy of her fingerprint.

Col   How on earth is computers one of my things?

Kath   You bought a Blu-Ray player and you were really into it.

An approach from off . . .

Col   Here she comes.

Kath   Right, now look like you weren't just trying to break into her computer.

In comes **Julie**, *dumping her gym bag.*

Julie   *Shwmae ffrindiau da.*

Col   Alright, love.

Kath   You look hungover. How was Gwenni?

There's something a little loaded to this, but **Julie** *ignores it.*

Julie   Oh you know. Same as always.

She picks up on an atmosphere between them.

You two fighting? Don't stop for me . . .

Kath   We weren't fighting.

Julie   (*to* **Col**)   Was she picking on you?

Col   You left your laptop on the floor and when I moved it, it woke up, and I saw –

There was a notification.

Julie *knows instantly what it is.*

Julie   Oh God. Right.

But she doesn't move to the laptop.

Kath   Are you gonna look?

Julie   Mm-hm.

Col   D'you want us to leave you alone?

Julie   No you're fine.

She's looking at them.

Col   You okay?

Julie *types a pin to unlock the laptop.*

Col   I thought it was fingerprints.

Julie   Fingerprint reader's broken.

She types. Then stops.

Kath   What?

Julie   Yep. It's there. It's the –

It's from Cambridge.

Kath   And?

She stops, pulls away from the laptop a little.

Julie   Can you do it?

Kath *grabs the laptop off her.*

Jabs at it. Clicks something.

Looks.

Kath   I mean I –

Col   Lemme see.

Kath *budges over a bit to let* **Col** *look.*

Col   Oh.

He reads.

And reads again.

Then he straightens up.

Goes over to **Julie**.

Wraps his arms around her.

She hugs him back.

Col   I am so proud of you.

Julie   Thanks, Dad.

Col   But I am gonna miss you so much.

It takes **Julie** *a second.*

Julie   What?

Col   When you're away up there in Cambridge.

Julie   What?

Kath   She's gotta get the grades first.

Julie   Sorry, *what?*

She moves, fast, to the laptop.

Col   Course she's gonna get the grades!

Julie   They offered me a place.

Kath   I know!

Julie   I've got a place, at Cambridge University.

Kath   . . . if you get an A star, an A star and an A.

Col   She can do that easy!

Kath *smiles.*

Kath   Oh God, she probably can . . .

Col   No one in our family's been to university, ever – and my daughter's going to Cambridge!

Julie   I haven't done it yet.

Kath   But you will. I'll see to that.

Col   How are you getting on with that, what was it relative moments?

Julie   Relativistic momentum.

Col   You cracked that now?

Julie   I think maybe only a dozen people in the world truly understand relativistic momentum, on a philosophical level.

Col   So you're gonna need that tutor, then.

Julie   Can't afford it, can we.

Col   You worry about the physics, I'll worry about the cash.

Julie   Dad . . .

Col   I'll do some overtime. Years I've been fooling your mum I'm a dab hand at DIY by always being too busy to do any. Let's not ruin it now.

Julie   Thanks, Dad.

Col   But we deserve a little celebration.

Kath   What's this gonna be, chippy tea?

Col   No, pushing the boat out tonight.

He's making to get off to work.

Julie   Not . . .

Col   Oh yeah.

Julie   Chinese from the Hot Wok?

Col   Yep. And I'm paying. Up to a tenner each.

He hugs her.

So proud of you, love.

Julie   Thanks, Dad.

He goes.

And as soon as he's gone, the mood shifts.

Kath   Well done, then.

Julie   Thanks.

Kath*'s waiting for* **Julie** *to say something. She doesn't.*

Kath   You and Gwenni up late were you?

Julie   Late-ish. Not stupid late, cos I'm not stupid.

Kath *looks at her.*

Kath   You gonna keep this up much longer?

Julie   Keep what up?

Kath   I text Gwenni's mum saying I hoped you weren't too much trouble.

Julie   My friend . . . had a childcare crisis and there was no one else to help, so I did.

Kath   Your friend had a . . .?

Julie   My friend Romy had a childcare crisis.

Using the phrase 'childcare crisis' is hilarious to her.

What?

Kath   What friends of yours have got kids? I mean Bethan's looked knocked-up since year 9 but still . . .

Julie   Nice bit of body shaming, Mum, well done.

Kath   So who's this Romy?

Julie   Got chatting at the library.

Kath   Goes to Willows does she?

Julie   It's a he.

Kath   And this . . . Romy, who's a he, had a childcare crisis. Did he.

Julie   Happens sometimes. To people with kids.

Kath   Really? Do fucking tell.

Julie   Can you not swear at me please?

Kath   So when you say, childcare crisis –

Julie   Okay. Fine.

Romy is a single dad. He's got an alcoholic mum. I said I'd go round look after Niamh for a couple of hours give him a bit of a break –

Kath   And why would you be doing that?

Julie   Yeah why would I do anything for anyone?

It's for my Community Challenge. Voluntary service in the community?

Ah yes, she gets it now. Why would I do anything for another human being except if it gets me into / uni –

Kath   And you had to do it on a school night?

Julie   The plan was I'd go round for two hours –

Kath   But you stayed all night.

Julie   D'you know what crisis means, Mum? It means unexpected, difficult, uhh . . . you know what I'll look it up –

Kath   You stayed all night, and you lied about it.

Julie   Because I knew you'd be like this, and you are being like this, so I should've just lied better shouldn't I –

Kath   I can still give you a clip round the ear, love.

Julie It's actually illegal for a parent to hit a child in Wales now?

Kath You're not a child.

Julie Then it's just assault.

Kath *closes her eyes.*

Julie Oh my God are you actually having to count to ten in your head so you don't go for me –

Kath's *steadied herself in spite of* **Julie** *trying to rile her.*

Kath So what was this crisis, love?

Julie Oh just. Romy's mum phoned, she was she didn't know where but Ely somewhere and Romy had to go and fetch her and I said, yeah, you go, I'll stay here with Nevey.

Kath Nevey's the baby.

Julie It's long for Niamh. I know it was not, like, the best thing to be doing, but – his mum could've got raped, if he'd left her there.

Kath And what was your offer again? A star, A star, A?

Julie The day I get an offer from Cambridge – and you're bollocking me about not working hard enough?

Kath And you and this Romy – that's all it is, you went round to help this once. There's nothing going on.

Julie No.

Kath Not at all?

Julie Am I not allowed a personal life?

Kath Right.

Julie Cos if that's how it is, you just say it. If that's a rule of the house now.

Kath I thought this might happen. I thought it and I hated myself for thinking it. But I thought it anyway.

Julie   What? What did Kath think?

Kath   That when it really came down to it – you would chicken out.

Julie   How am I chickening out?

Kath   Listen, you can shag who you like / once you get to uni –

Julie (*under* **Kath**)   Jesus Christ . . .

Kath   – but just for now, will you please keep it together. I know you couldn't care less what I think –

Julie   – nah course I don't –

Kath   – but at least think about your dad.

Julie   What about him?

Kath *doesn't answer.*

Julie   What?

Kath   You hear him coughing every morning.

Julie   Hard not to.

Kath   There you are then.

Julie   He said that's from smoking sixty a day in the eighties.

Kath   You think of all the crap he's breathing every day in that steel mill.

Julie   That's why his chest's bad?

Kath   I am on at him every bloody week to pack it in and we'll manage somehow but no. He keeps going. He doesn't care what it does to him so long as you get everything you need.

Please, love. Don't take the piss out of that.

Julie   Jesus, you are freaking me out now.

Kath   Promise me you're not going to see this boy again.

Julie   Seriously?

Kath *waits.*

Julie   Okay, I promise –

– I'm not gonna do anything, to distract me from A levels. Okay?

Kath *takes this in. Gives up. She's tried to get through to her.*

Kath   Well, there we are then.

She moves past **Julie***, stops, kisses her on the top of the head.*

Kath   Well done, love. We're really proud of you.

She goes.

Scene Five

Barb*'s flat.* **Barb** *leads* **Julie** *in.*

Barb   It's nice to finally meet you, love.

Julie   Yeah and you.

Barb   Pretty little thing and all.

Julie   I do alright with an hour and a half on hair and make-up.

Barb   You was an hour and a half on that?

Julie   No, I was just –

Barb   Cos I was gonna say –

Julie   It was just a joke really.

Barb   – you look nice but not an hour and a bloody half.

Julie   No, well.

It's not the first time we've met actually.

Barb   No?

Julie   Cos I was here the night Romy had to fetch you back from Ely. I was here, looking after Niamh. But you probably don't remember.

Barb   Well, if you've come to see Romy he's out with his other woman.

Julie   Sorry, what?

Barb   I'm teasing you I am, love. Niamh gets colicky in the evenings and only pushing her in the pram'll shut her up. He says the industrial estate gets quiet once everyone's gone home, so that's where he goes. He must look mental pushing a pram round and round there, just him and the prossies.

Julie   It was actually you I wanted to talk to, Barb.

She's just a smidge forced-casual about using **Barb***'s first name.*

Barb   Is it?

Julie   If you got five minutes.

Barb   Well, sit yourself down then. Something to drink?

Julie   Bit early for me.

Barb   I meant a cup of tea.

No she didn't.

Julie   No I'm alright I think.

Barb   So what did you wanna talk about?

Julie   I don't know if Romy's said but I'm trying to get into Cambridge.

Barb   No he's never said nothing about that.

Julie   No?

A tiny smile on **Barb***'s face.*

Julie   You're teasing me again.

Barb   I am! I bloody am and all! No he has mentioned like once or twice or ten million times how clever you are.

Julie   So I got my offer through from uni and I was gonna have a night out with the girls to celebrate? And I'd really like Romy to come.

Barb *shifts.*

Julie   And I know Romy asked you if you would maybe babysit Niamh for him, so he could come out?

Barb   He has. And I said no.

Julie   And I get it, you've brought up your kids, complete respect for that, and you let Romy stay here and that's great –

Barb   You get it do you?

Julie   I get why you have a limit on what you do / cos you've gotta –

Barb   I don't help him more with Nevey, because he shouldn't have bloody taken her. He's too –

– he can't do it.

Julie   He does it every day.

Barb   Babies are a piece of piss. You put them down, they stay put. You wait till she starts –

He's at the end of his tether now. He can't cope.

Julie   Maybe he could if he had a bit more help.

Barb   And who's gonna give him all this help – oh me?

Well, I suppose I could. But I'm not gonna be here forever am I.

Julie   Okay. When I've done babysitting I've had six quid an hour, but like cos you're a grown-up I thought maybe ten was fairer?

Barb   What's this?

Julie   If I hire you to babysit, maybe Romy could come out for my birthday?

Barb   You wanna pay me? To look after my own grand-daughter?

Julie   I'm very sorry if I offended you.

It's just when I got my offer through my dad was like, right, you didn't do anything for your birthday cos you were studying for your mocks, so – have a night off now, you deserve it.

And I thought – Romy never gets a night off does he.

Barb   That's because babies never take / a night off –

Julie   And I think he probably deserves one. Don't you?

Barb *softens a little.*

Barb   So what're you doing then? For your celebration?

Julie   Aw just – just going out with the girls, nothing special.

Barb   You think Romy'd like a night out with the girls?

Julie   I think he'll bloody love it, little flirt.

Barb   You're a funny girl. Lots of people don't like that. I do.

Alright then. If you're paying, I'll babysit. For one night only.

Julie   Seriously?

Barb   He won't be getting another night off for years, so you make sure he has a good one.

Julie   Oh my God I definitely will.

Barb *looks at her – she let a bit too much of her actual intent slip through then.*

Julie Anyway. Thank you so much, Mrs Jones.

Barb You're welcome, love.

Julie No, I really appreciate it.

I best be going then.

Barb Take care, God bless.

Just as she's leaving.

And you be kind to my boy. When you've had enough of him.

Scene Six

Julie *calls* **Romy**.

Julie And?

Romy Just having to run through a couple things with Mum.

Julie Listen, mate. If you're alright leaving me on my own then that's your look-out. I gotta tell you though . . . I am looking pretty . . . you know.

Romy What d'you mean, on your own? Where's the girls?

Julie Just get a move on.

She ends the call.

Noise outside.

Barb (*from off*) Alright, love?

She enters. **Romy** *can tell the second he sees her that all is not well.*

Romy You're late.

Barb Oh hiya, Mum, how're you, how was your day? Fine thanks very much, / love, thanks for –

Romy You said you'd be here half-eight.

Barb And I was going to be. And then –

Romy   You are kidding me . . .

Barb   – I bumped into an old friend, the evening took a turn.

Romy   How much have you had?

Barb   Wanna smell my breath?

Romy   Christ no.

Barb   We had a drink to say hello, a drink to say goodbye.

That was it. Two drinks.

Romy   Two drinks doesn't even hit the sides for you.

Barb   Yes alright it was hello goodbye and the odd little sip in between.

Oh my God your face. I'm *fine*.

Romy   I asked for one night.

Barb   Are you telling me I can't be trusted my with own grand-daughter?

Romy   See that's how I know you're hammered. You have to be to call her your grand-daughter.

Barb   Okay. Okay. I had more than I meant to. Alright? And I shouldn't've. I'm admitting it.

I made a mistake. People do.

But don't make me out to be an arsehole because I made one little mistake because I am not, I am not that, Romy, and you bloody know it.

Cos my friend was like – let's make a night of it! But I said no. I made a promise. So home I come. To your fucking miserable face and your fucking miserable baby.

Romy   My fucking miserable baby? She was your grand-daughter two minutes ago.

Barb   Well, Christ, is she? That'd be just like you, get
lumbered bringing up another bloke's kid cos some slapper
told you she was yours.

Romy   Why don't you fuck off.

Barb   What did you say to me?

He doesn't repeat it.

I try and do one nice thing for you. And this is the thanks
I get.

Romy   Julie told me she's paying you. So don't bullshit me.

Barb *grabs her coat.*

Romy   What you doing now?

Barb   What d'you think? You think I'm gonna sit round
here to be insulted?

Romy   You said you'd babysit.

Barb   That was before you called me a cunt.

Romy   Well, I actually didn't.

Barb   Yeah you did, Romy. Yeah you fuckin did. So let's see
how you get on without me, shall we?

She goes.

Romy *sits.*

Then picks up his phone.

Julie   Finally!

Romy   Listen –

Julie   Guess where I am.

Romy *goes to* **Barb**'s *room.*

Julie   I know I said Tiger Tiger with the girls, but . . . that
was the cover story. But actually it's just me. And actually I'm
down the bay.

I'm in that hotel right on the water. And –

– I'm here cos there was an offer fifty quid for a room and so
– I got us. A room.

Romy *walks back in, carrying the Moses basket. With* **Niamh** *in it.*

Julie   – so we're gonna drink and talk and laugh and watch
the sun go down over the sea. Just the two of us.

And then we're gonna go upstairs, to our room. And then
. . . well, you're used to a girl keeping you up all night, aren't
you.

He puts the Moses basket down.

Romy   Oh my Christ.

Julie   So see you soon then.

Romy   Yeah be there now.

She ends the call.

He stands.

He doesn't know what to do.

He goes to the Moses basket.

Looks down at **Niamh** *sleeping.*

Goes over to the fridge. Gets out a bottle.

Puts it down in the basket next to her.

Kisses his fingers, presses them to her head.

Looks down at her.

Then really quickly puts a jacket on, moves off, goes.

Door to the street opens, closes.

A pause.

Romy *comes back into the room.*

Throws his jacket off.

Slumps down somewhere.

Romy   Fuck.

Scene Seven

Barb's *flat. Empty.*

Romy *enters, dressed as we last saw him.*

And following him **Julie**, *dressed as we last saw her but with a jacket over the top.*

Julie   So this room. The view was . . . amazing. The sea, the lights, the waves, little tinkling from the boats in the marina. But it wasn't the view.

Romy   What was it then?

Julie   There was the bed. Super king size.

Romy   Bit of space.

Julie   Yeah, space to . . . anything you want. but it wasn't the bed.

Romy   It wasn't?

Julie   It was the wet room.

Romy   The hell is a wet room?

Julie   It is every bit as pervy as it sounds.

So there's a lot of space. To be in the shower. The water running over you. And to just – express yourself.

Romy   You look amazing.

Julie   Oh I know.

She gets out a present.

I got this for Nevey.

Romy *opens it. A board book called* Quantum Physics for Babies.

Romy   That's good of you, yeah.

Julie   Isn't it.

A beat.

I had to lie to my mum and dad, about where I was going –

Romy (*under her*)   Yeah I know –

She's not going to be interrupted.

Julie   – I had to get Gwenni to lie to her mum, to cover for me. I had to find the offer for the hotel. I had to pay for the hotel. I had to pay your mum to babysit. All that, for you. So you could have one brilliant night. One night, me not worrying about exams, you not worrying about –

Romy   My daughter.

Julie   Yes: for one night.

Romy   With me there's always Nevey too.

Julie   Of course I know that and that's why I got your mum –

Romy   And my mum turned up hammered and then stropped off back down the pub. And all that other stuff . . . Thank you. Really. But –

The board book.

You get me this, for me to read to Nevey? I can barely fuckin read it myself.

You know I can't.

Does she?

Julie   How come you can't read?

Romy   Was always shit at it. I hated school, cos I was shit at it. So I stopped going.

Julie   Your mum should've made you go.

Romy   Should she.

They look at each other.

You do all this stuff to fix things for me and it's so – kind of you. But it's not just me. It's my life. It's everything.

Julie   I can't fix everything, can I?

Romy   No. Not even you.

Julie   I was really trying, Romy. Cos when it's just the two of us –

Romy   I know.

Julie   You're the only person I can say anything I like, what I actually think, what I actually feel, and you listen.

Romy   But it's never just the two of us. It's the world as well.

Julie   It feels like it's just the two of us. Sometimes.

Romy   Yeah it does. But that's just how it feels. And how it feels is a fuckin lie.

You may's well head back to your posh hotel, enjoy your posh bed.

Cos that's where you're going, in the end.

But she doesn't.

Julie   And is that it then? With us?

Romy   Well, what's the point? You with your relativistic momentum and I can't even read a baby book.

Julie   Right. Okay.

She goes to him. Takes the book from his hand. Opens it.

You see this? The 't'? Makes a 'tuh' sound. And the 'h' makes a 'huh' sound usually, but together they make 'th'.

Romy   What the fuck you doing?

Julie   You taught me how to feed a baby. So I owe you. I'll teach you this.

He can't answer.

He grabs her, kisses her.

Then she gets back to the book.

Julie   Right. So this next one –

He takes the book.

Romy   Teach me later.

Kisses her again.

She gives in to it.

Act Two

Scene One

Night.

The Splott foreshore – or Splott beach, depending who you ask.

Julie *and* **Romy** *are picking their way across the bricks and pebbles, carrying* **Niamh**'s *buggy between them.*

They get to where they're going and set the buggy down.

Romy   Well, this was a shit idea.

Julie   Who doesn't like the beach.

Romy   The shittest beach in the world.

Julie's *getting out binoculars. She's got an astronomy app on her phone – she's scanning across the horizon with her phone, looking for something.*

Romy   D'you ever wonder why there's all this bricks and metal and . . . broken toilets and crap.

She finds what she's looking for.

Julie   Okay. It's gonna come from this direction.

She's looking through binoculars. She sees something.

Julie   There it is now – see?

Gives the binoculars to **Romy**, *points, tracking something in the sky.*

Julie   That's it. The International Space Station. D'you see the solar panels?

Romy   I dunno, do I?

Julie   Little sticky-out bits.

Romy   Okay yeah.

Julie   There it goes. Bye, space station. Bye.

And there's actual people on that little dot, right now.

Romy   I'd love to have a go at floating, in space.

Julie   You feel like you're falling, all the time.

Romy   Okay let's not bother then.

Julie   That's why people are sick all the time when they get there.

Romy   And where's the Milky Way?

Julie   It's –

She looks, checks the view in her phone.

Julie   – well, it's sort of there.

Romy   It's bloody not.

Julie   There's too much light to see it. I'll take you up the mountains one day, you'll see the stars, you'll see the Milky Way, it will blow your mind.

Romy   Or it'll freeze my arse off.

Julie   It can do both, no problem.

She shifts.

Julie   D'you wanna know something funny?

Romy   Course.

Julie   You remember that time we didn't have a really filthy night in the St David's Hotel?

Romy   Yeah. And we ended up having a really filthy night in my mum's flat.

Julie   Yeah and remember the fourth time.

Romy   I didn't think I'd have the strength but – oh yes I did.

Julie   But what we didn't have was a condom by then.

Romy   What is the funny thing, by the way? You said there was a funny thing.

Julie I dunno if is this exactly funny but I was on the settee and you were kneeling between my legs really.

And I think I was a bit distracted by – you. And you said but we haven't got another condom and I said lemme have a think about the dates, and I did the sums and I said yeah okay we're fine.

Romy That is not what you said.

Julie I know it's not but I'm not saying that stuff now.

She waits for him to get it. He doesn't.

Julie So I might be pregnant.

Romy What d'you mean you might be?

Julie I definitely am. Unless there was a whole batch of dodgy tests at Tesco's –

Romy Are you alright?

Julie Course. It's a perfectly natural state. I'm probably at the prime age for it, biologically speaking.

Romy No I mean are you alright, like in your head.

Julie Yeah.

Romy I'm really sorry.

Julie Sorry for what?

Romy It's my fault.

Julie I dunno if fault is a helpful notion right now. And I was there too.

Romy So what are we gonna do?

Julie What are *we* gonna do?

She looks at him.

It's fine.

It's not fine it's a pain but – it'll *be* fine.

Romy   Have you had one before?

Julie   Like . . . an abortion? No.

Romy   I'll come in with you.

Julie   You don't, go in.

Romy   I thought it was like an operation.

Julie   They give you pills.

You're not, like, in hospital or anything.

Romy   You're just . . . walking around?

Julie   Well, probably not cos you know it's coming.

Romy   And what do you –

– do with it?

Julie   Do with it?

Romy   If it just –

Like with the – if it just comes out of you.

Julie   I dunno.

Wrap it up in toilet paper and put it in the bin.

Or flush it down the toilet, I dunno.

Romy   Fuck.

Julie   Yeah.

Romy   I'm really sorry.

Julie   Me too.

A silence between them.

Julie   Can I have Nevey?

Romy   Yeah. Won't that be weird?

Julie   Weird holding a baby when I'm talking about – I dunno she just makes me feel better.

Romy *comes over. They transfer* **Niamh.**

Julie *buries her head into* **Niamh.**

Romy *watches.*

Romy   Crap thing to have to put up with while you're studying.

Julie   It'll be fine.

Romy   It's not gonna help though.

Julie   Thing with me is I get too into it, like just hyper-focused so actually it'll be good for me to have to take a break, put down the books, nip up the road for a cheeky abortion.

Now that is funny.

Romy   Is it.

Julie   You're laughing on the inside.

Romy   On the inside I'm feeling really shit you have to go through this.

Julie   Just remember it is me going through it, so let's not get to point where I'm comforting you, cos of how bad you feel for me.

Romy   No, fair enough.

They sit a bit.

Julie   All these years we've been tramping round the same streets. And we meet now. And we get together now. And cos it's now, I get pregnant, and like obviously – it's a bad thing, we get rid of it.

Romy   Well, yeah.

Julie   But if it was ten years' time, and we were together, and I got pregnant – we'd be like celebrating. It'd be a good thing.

It's just weird.

Romy   Yeah.

Not like you'd ever be back here, in ten years' time though is it.

Julie   Well.

I dunno. I might be here doing my post-grad.

Romy   The hell's your post-grad?

Julie   If you wanna be a physicist it's not just the one degree.

After your first one you go on and do another one, a doctorate. In some really specific bit of physics.

Romy   And you might do that here?

Julie   Cardiff Uni've got a decent physics department. I put them down as one of my back-up choices.

Romy   What d'you mean?

Julie   Like when you apply for uni, you put a few different places. And you accept one offer as your main offer. But then you can have another one as your back-up. In case you don't get the grades you need for your main offer. So, like, Cambridge asked for A star, A star, A, which is, like, okay, I'm gonna have to work for that. But Cardiff asked for two Cs. Which is a piece of piss.

Two Cs is really low for them, they must've really wanted me.

Romy *takes this on.*

Romy   Can I have her?

They swap **Niamh.**

Romy   So – like if you hadn't got an offer from Cambridge, you might've just gone to uni here?

Julie   Yeah.

Romy   And not gone away at all?

Julie   No.

What?

Romy   Just I didn't know that was like an option.

Julie   Well, it was like a back-up.

Romy   You could study what you wanna study, and do it here?

Julie   Yeah.

Romy   And it would be as good? Studying here, it would be as good as going to Cambridge?

Julie   It's all the same physics.

Romy   Okay.

Julie   What?

Romy   So why don't you stay here?

Julie   Well, because –

Romy   Why don't you study here, and stay with me?

She doesn't know how to say what she wants to say; or what she wants to say.

Romy   Is it you want to leave? Like I'll do for a few months and a story to tell when you get to uni / but –

Julie   No, fucking no.

You know that's not it. Don't you.

Romy   Because if you stayed, all that stuff from ten years' time – we could do that now.

Julie   How could we?

Romy   You go to uni, here, and do your whole mad scientist thing. And I look after Niamh. And our baby.

Julie   No way am I ready to have a kid.

Romy   Your body's making one right now.

Julie   Yeah but only / because of – [a mistake]

Romy   Niamh was a mistake. And she turned into the best thing in my life.

Like if you'd thought about getting together with someone now, would you have said – single dad, brilliant.

Julie   Obviously not.

Romy   But how d'you feel about it now?

Would you rather I didn't have her? Or are you glad I do?

Julie   Well, obviously I –

She dries up.

Romy   Say it.

Julie   Am I allowed to?

I love her, don't I.

Romy   We can make a family. We basically already have.

It's just – do you want to?

Julie   I mean – no.

I mean – yes. There's a version where –

But what if it goes wrong?

Romy   Things go wrong whatever you do.
    Like, Cambridge. You might hate it.

Julie   Things could go wrong with us.

Romy   Because they always can.
    But if things always can go wrong
    Then you might as well
    Go for everything you want, and see
    How much you can get.

And I can see now you're freaking out a bit –

Julie   I am not fucking freaking out –

Romy   A little bit.

Julie   I don't know how to
Bring up a kid.

Romy   I'll teach you.
We'll teach each other.
Our baby'll teach us.

Julie   Do you think I can?

Romy   All the time at soft play people think you're Niamh's mum.

Julie   Yeah I know they / do –

Romy   I'm not gonna tell you what to do.
But I'm begging you:
Don't go along with what you've always thought
And tell yourself you've got to carry on the same
Because life fucking ambushes you again and again
And what you think is going to ruin you –
Well, it does, it wrecks you fair play
But you climb out the ruins and you're someone else.
And you're maybe someone new.
So I'm just asking you to really think
What do you want?
Because you can leave, you can go.
Or you can stay, and have me, and Niamh
And the universe; and our baby,
If you want to.
But do you want to?

She doesn't know.

And then –

Julie   I want us.
I want you.

Scene Two

Kath *and* **Col**'s *place.*

Julie *has just explained her new plans.*

Julie   So.
I'm not giving up studying.
I'm not giving up my degree. I'm just
Going to do it here, while
Romy is the main carer for our baby.

Col   You finished?

Julie   Yes. Thank you for listening
And giving me space to explain myself.

Col   Can we talk now?

Julie   Yes / you can –

Kath   You stupid, stupid / little idiot –

Julie   Thanks for that, Mum, constructive as usual.
Dad you got anything? And please don't say you're going
to kill him.

Col   I haven't said anything.

Julie   But when you do, don't be all 'I'm gonna bloody kill
him' cos, honestly – just do better.

Col   You're telling *me* to do better?

Kath   How far along?

Julie   Hardly at all. Seven weeks-ish?

Kath   Seven.

Julie   What?

Kath's *just staring at her.*

Julie   I'm a bit all over the place sometimes.

Kath   Right.

Col We need to get you in to see Dr Kabeer now –

Julie Already have been.

Col What'd she say?

Julie That I'm up the duff.

Col I was in about my blood pressure yesterday she didn't say a thing to me –

Kath She's not allowed to.

Col – my own daughter? Good God . . .

Kath How could you be so fucking stupid . . .

Julie We were being careful.

Kath There's being careful and there's making bloody sure.

Julie D'you want me to cry? If I cry will you at least be nice to me?

Kath I wouldn't think so, no.

Julie I have thought it about how all this can work, I'm not stupid.

Kath You got yourself knocked up, you are bloody stupid.

Julie Physics and Astronomy at Cardiff is very highly rated.

Kath You think you're gonna do a degree, with a new baby?

Julie Parenthood should not hold women back any more than it does men.

Kath *stares at her. Then just laughs.*

Kath You haven't got a fucking *clue*.

Julie What I have got is a partner who's going to support me in carrying on my education with a new baby –

Kath What if she's premature?

Julie Well, I suppose –

Kath   What if she's in special care and she doesn't come home from hospital for weeks? Then what? You're going to uni with your little baby on her own in an incubator?

Julie   Then – we'll have to / deal with that –

Kath   Things happen with babies that you don't see coming.

Julie   Well, if I can't see things coming then I can't plan how to deal with them, can I.

Kath   You deal with them by not having a bloody baby when you're eighteen, that's how.

Julie   If she is premature, then me and Romy will take turns being in hospital with her.

Kath   And what if she gets ill.

Julie   Well, again, me / and Romy –

Kath   What if she doesn't sleep? What if she's colicky?

Julie   I dunno yet –

Kath   What if they cock up the birth and you're incontinent, how will that be on Freshers' Week?

Julie   What if they what?

Kath   Or what if everything's fine but you love her and you just can't bear not to be with her for every second of the start of her life?

Julie   I don't know!

Kath   No you don't.

You see?

Julie *says nothing.*

Kath *holds off.*

Julie   You're right.

I've not done this before, there are / things I –

Kath It's just too much, love. For anyone.

Julie's *taking it in.*

Kath Now look. You don't have to go through this alone.

Julie Thank you.

Kath I mean d'you want me to – when you talk to Romy, shall I come / with you –

Julie No. Thank you.

Kath Okay. But everything else. I'm with you. Alright?

Julie You're right. It's too much. I hadn't thought of all this stuff.

So what I'm going to do is, I'm gonna defer my place at uni for a year.

Col What's that mean?

Kath Push it back a year.

Col And they'll just let you do that, will they?

Julie So whatever happens, I've got a year to cope with it. I've got a year to get used to having a baby. And then I'll start uni not this September but the September after.

Next question.

Kath Is this some kind of breakdown? Is the work just too much?

Julie I'm fine. You look a bit stressed though. Shall I crack open a bottle for you?

Kath Do not even start . . .

Julie People think I'm Niamh's mum.

Kath But you're not.

Julie I feed her, change her, *cwtsh* her.

I do whatever she needs.

Is that not being her mum?

Kath   Not after three bloody months, no.

You have to earn it.

Julie   And I will.

Kath *can't answer her.*

Julie   I know it's a shock, so what I think is, why don't you take some time to let it soak in before we really talk / about it –

Col   Where d'you think you're gonna live?

Julie   There's some family accommodation at the uni. It's / subsidised as well –

Col   And you can move into that.

Julie   Yeah.

I mean – obviously not straight away. Not if I defer. You've gotta be at the uni, before they let you into uni halls.

Col   Okay.

Okay.

Julie   What?

Col   The last six years we've done everything we can to get you to university. You've been saying you want to go to university and do physics since you were twelve.

Julie   That's what I said when I was twelve –

Col   And when you were thirteen, and fourteen, and fifteen –

Julie   And now I'm saying different.

Col   Of all the things. To give it up for a boy.

Julie   I love him.

I do.

Col   You do *now*.

Julie   How old was Mum when she had me?

Col   You've got choices we didn't have.

Julie   And I'm making them. For the first time ever, I'm doing what I want. And look at you.

Col   Right. I've heard you out. I've listened.

I can't let you do this.

Julie   How're you gonna stop me?

Col   I want you to leave.

Julie   What d'you mean?

Col   This is what you wanna do? Fine.

You and Romy want your little family? Fine.

But you're not doing it here. You can get out.

Julie   Where'm I supposed to go?

Col   Up to you.

Julie   What if I end up on the streets?

Col   Then – that's a really terrible place to have a baby.

Julie   I can't believe you're doing this. You're not.

You're not really.

Kath?

For once, **Kath** *doesn't know what to say.* **Julie** *turns on* **Col** *again.*

Julie   You're making me choose, you or Romy?

And you think I'll choose you?

You're the ones that haven't got a clue.

Col   I think you are clever, and funny, and stubborn as hell,

But you are soft, love. You're soft cos we spent years

Seeing to it that nothing in your life

Would make you hard.

You've got what it takes to learn things

I'll never have a clue about.

But you have not got what it takes

To bring up a baby, in a bedsit, in Splott.

And if you can't see that then –

– I've gotta show you.

Pack tonight please. Leave first thing.

Julie   Dad, come on / I –

Col *gets up and leaves.*

Julie   Mum?

If I actually do this, if I actually pack, can't you see
How embarrassing it's gonna be for him
When he calms down?

Kath   You heard your dad, love.

It's time for you to go.

Scene Three

Barb'*s flat.*

Julie and **Romy** *coming into the flat. Loaded down with* **Julie**'*s stuff.* **Julie** *with her wheeled suitcase and a rucksack and more.*

Barb   So what's all this kerfuffle then?

Julie   My mum's having one of her rages. Time of life I reckon.

Barb   Is it.

Julie   What's pathetic is, she gets my dad to do the dirty work? So it's him saying I've got to go?

Barb   Go where, love?

Julie   They couldn't give a shit. Just go.

Barb   They've chucked you out? No disrespect to your parents, Julie, I'm sure they're lovely people – but I'd eat broken glass before I'd throw mine on the streets.

Julie   It is bad, isn't it.

Barb   Blood is blood. It's all we got in this life.

Julie   I know. (*To* **Romy**.) So can you give me a hand getting all this to Mabli's?

Barb   Hold on, hold on, what you on about?

Julie   My friend said I could stay with / her for a bit –

Barb   You're not going to no Mandy's! You're stopping here!

Julie   But how can I, / Barb, there's –

Barb   You're round here half the time anyway. You're near everything you know. You're near that pillock, which is where it seems like you want to be.

(*To* **Romy**.) Oi, pillock, you wouldn't mind, would you?

Romy   . . . no. Course not.

Barb   Course he bloody wouldn't!

It'd be a squash but – the more the merrier.

Julie   Are you sure?

Barb   Stay as long as you like.

Julie   What d'you think?

Romy   'S up to you.

I think yes, obviously!

Julie   Then yes. Yes please, Barb, that's very good of you. You'll hardly know I'm here.

Barb   Family's family, love.

Julie   Thank you. That's –

And not quiet sure she's going to do it, and not quite sure it's going to be accepted, she goes over –

– and gives **Barb** *a hug.*

Julie   Shall I go out get us chips, to celebrate me not being on the street?

Barb   Well, I was gonna cook but – haddock if they got it, cod if they don't.

Julie   Romy – jumbo sausage?

Straight face.

Romy   You know me.

Julie   See you in a bit.

She heads off.

Barb   What?

Romy   That's nice of you. Letting her stay.

Barb   I'm a nice person, Romy.

Romy   I thought you didn't like her.

Barb   She's a stuck-up cow, what's to like.

But what kind of life will Nevey have with a clever girl like that as her step-mum. And what kind of life will she have if she's stuck with the two of us, eh.

She's staying, love. She's staying as long as we can keep her.

Scene Four

Barb's *flat.*

Barb *leads* **Kath** *in.*

Kath   See I like this, it's very cosy.

Barb   Bloody is now with your daughter squashed in here! I'm teasing I am, love.

She's in the other room. I say the other room, my room. I let her go in there do her revising, get a bit of peace and quiet.

Kath   Don't disturb her if she's working, I don't need to actually –

But **Barb** *is continuing towards the door regardless. So* **Kath** *stops.*

Barb   Julie? Out you come love, visitor for you.

She'll be out now.

Kath   I am very grateful to you, for taking / her in –

Barb   Least I could do love. Least I could do.

Julie *enters cheery enough. Till she sees* **Kath.**

Julie   I was working.

Kath   I did say not to / bother you –

Barb   Your mum's popped round, that's nice of her isn't it.

Julie   She only lives round the corner.

Barb   Still, she could just as easily not.

Julie   What's up? Wifi need fixing does it?

Kath   Just came to say hello.

Julie   Hello. Anything else?

Kath   Couple things I thought you'd need.

She's got a couple of bags for life.

Julie   How you're doing then, Mum?

Kath   How'd you think, love?

Julie   I think rattling round the house without me you're both loving it.

Barb   Julie – don't be a twat there's a good girl.

An odd moment for **Kath**.

Kath   And how are you?

Julie   Like you're bothered.

Barb   You like a drink, Kath? Tea, coffee?

Julie *and* **Kath** *staring at each other.*

Barb   I was gonna have a little glass of red.

Kath (*to* **Julie**)   You know I am.

Barb   It's a bit of a throat stripper but –

Kath   Actually, I wouldn't mind.

Julie   Drinking in the afternoon now are you?

Barb   It's evening, love.

Kath   Well, why not.

Julie *breaks away, finds something to do.*

Barb   Sit yourself down, Kath. If you can find space.

Kath *finds somewhere to settle.*

Barb *pours a couple of glasses. Hands one to* **Kath**.

Barb   Kids. Fucking nightmare.

Kath   I'll drink to that.

Barb   Cheers.

Kath   Cheers.

Takes a sip.

Kath   How's revision?

Julie   Literally all you care about.

Barb *sighs –* **Kath** *meets her gaze.*

Barb   Give up, I would.

Kath   How long've you been here?

Barb   Couple of years. Was in a house in Adeline Street when the kids were little but this suited me better. You Moorland Road?

Kath   Yeah.

Barb   Lovely houses them. Do you get many trains on that line?

Kath   Not for weeks and one'll come at five in the morning.

Barb   And you sent her to Welsh school. Keeps her away from all the riff raff round here I suppose.

Kath   That's not why we / sent her –

Barb   I woulda sent Romy to Welsh school, but he's too thick.

Julie   He's not thick.

Barb   You say that, but you fancy him.

Kath   So how is the work going, love?

Barb   Don't you worry about her, she's never off that bloody laptop.

Julie   How d'you think it's going, Mum?

Kath   I think –

Anyway you have these.

She hands over a bag for life.

Kath   And I'll be off.

Julie   Well nice to see you, Mum.

Kath   You know you can call in, any time.

Julie   Doesn't feel like I can.

Kath   Dad sends his love.

Julie   Are you joking?

Kath   Why would I be joking?

Barb   Haven't got a clue, have they?

Kath   No. She doesn't.

Barb   Tell you what – this red's gone right through me. Excuse me a sec.

She leaves them.

Kath   Are you alright here?

Julie   If I say I'm not, what then.

Kath   Are you?

Julie   I'm fine, thanks.

Kath   Not mad about the way she talks to you.

Julie   How's she talk to me?

Kath   The 'don't be a twat' stuff.

Julie   She thought I was being a twat, she told me so. She talks to me like I'm an adult.

Kath   No one's gonna be angry at you, or laugh at you, if that's what's stopping you.

Julie   Stopping me what?

Kath   You don't have to let a mistake ruin your whole life.

Julie   I haven't made a mistake. Dad made a bloody mistake and you let him.

Kath   You look shattered.

Julie   I am a bit tired yeah.

Kath   Not great for your exams.

Julie   I'll be alright.

Barb *returns.*

Barb   You know when you think you've got to, and then it turns out you can't? Worries me sometimes.

Kath   See you then, love.

Barb   Off already is it?

Kath   Probably best.

Barb   Call round, any time you want.

Kath   Thank you, I will.

She gets out a purse, counts out some notes.

Julie   Christ, do you think you're gonna buy / me off.

But **Kath** *hands the notes to* **Barb***.*

Kath   That's to cover her keep.

Barb   Thank you, lovely. She's got a bloody appetite on her, I'll say that!

Kath   And anything you need for her, let me know.

Barb   I'll make sure I do.

She leads **Kath** *off.*

Julie *waits.*

Barb *returns.*

Barb   Well.

She gets out the money. Counts off a single note.

Barb   You can have that. Rest I need – no offence but you're eating me out of house and home.

Julie   You should've said.

Barb   I just have.

She upset you?

Julie   More annoyed me really.

Barb   Yeah. They're annoying, mums. So Romy's always telling me.

She gets a glass.

Barb   Have a drink, take your mind off it.

Julie   You know I'm pregnant?

Barb   You're allowed one.

Julie   I'll be all fuzzy headed then won't be able to concentrate.

Barb   Fuck's sake.

She necks half what she poured for **Julie**.

Barb   Barely a mouthful left, you think you can handle that?

Julie *picks up the glass.*

Julie   I reckon.

Barb*'s watching the way* **Julie** *sits.*

Barb   Tits sore?

Julie   Bloody hell yeah.

Barb   Little bugger's ruining you already. But don't worry, when your – what is it – pelvic girdle starts giving you gyp that'll take your mind off the sore tits.

Julie   What's my pelvic girdle?

Barb   Oh, love.

Julie   What is it?

Barb   Well, I don't really know. But –

She stands – sort of gyrates, feeling how her legs connect to her abdomen.

Barb   It's like when the baby grows, it stretches you all out so much round here – it's like your legs are a little bit dislocated the whole time?

She lifts her glass.

Cheers!

Julie Yeah, cheers.

She takes a sip. **Barb** *tops up her glass.*

Julie Barb!

Barb Leave it then.

Julie You put it in front of me I'm gonna drink it aren't I.

Barb If you can't see a drink and not put it away, you've got problems, love. I'm serious now.

I'm not serious, I'm joking, I'm the same myself – if it's there, it's not gonna be there for long.

But then again I'm not pregnant. Far as I know.

Julie I half really want it and it's half making me feel like I'm gonna puke.

Barb It is cheap shit, fair play.

She takes a drink.

Did you think she was gonna ask you to come home?

Julie Yes, cos that's what a normal person would do. But then no, cos she's not a normal person she's my mum.

She takes a drink.

Barb 'S that Romy?

Julie Was it?

It was. **Romy** *enters, with* **Niamh**.

Julie How is she?

Romy Grizzling.

Julie She dirty, she hungry?

Romy Obviously I checked the obvious things.

Julie   Shall I give her a bottle?

Romy   Aye, go on.

Barb   Julie's mum was round, dropping off stuff.

Romy   How was she?

Julie   The same.

Romy   Bad as that.

He's seen the glass by now. **Barb**'s *getting a bottle.*

Romy   You been drinking?

Julie   I'm allowed one a week.

Barb   Shall I give her a feed, just to see?

Romy   Thanks, Mum.

Barb *takes* **Niamh***, goes.*

Romy   You get much done?

Julie   Not that much, no.

Romy   Just you said you needed to revise so I kept her out long as I could.

Julie   Your mum was on she wanted company.

Romy   Tell her you need to work.

Julie   While I'm living in her flat?

Romy   Well, either you need to work, or you don't.

She's firing up the laptop.

Julie   It is hard sometimes to concentrate, you know?

Romy   Like when you're a couple of glasses of wine down?

Julie   Barely had a mouthful.

Though my head feels full of itchy mud and the screen is burning my eyes.

Romy   Then switch it off.

Julie   Got too much to get through.

From next door, **Niamh** *starts crying.*

Barb (*re-entering*)   Romy can you give me a hand?

Julie   She's grumbling for you she is.

Romy   She's grumbling cos I kept her out, longer than I should've done and we're both freezing.

Julie   Did I ask you to do that?

Romy   You said you needed time. So I gave you time, and you sat chatting.

Julie   That make you feel better, saying that to me?

Romy   No, it makes me feel worse.

Barb   It's not colic.

Romy   What is it then?

Barb   Feel in her mouth.

Romy *does.*

Romy   What'm I feeling?

Barb   That little like ridge on her gums? That's a tooth coming through. She's teething.

Romy   Oh shit.

Julie   What does that mean?

Barb   It means a tooth is cutting its way through her gums. And it hurts.

He takes **Niamh**.

Barb   Give her a finger to chew on, you used to like that.

Romy *tries.* **Niamh** *quiets.*

Barb   She's not a little baby anymore, is she. She's growing up.

She watches **Niamh** *a moment.*

Barb   Right. I've done what I can. She's all yours.

She goes.

Julie   I'm not gonna get a thing done am I.

Romy   You said you had a headache anyway, give up for tonight, get some sleep and then –

Julie   But I got loads of stuff to get through.

Romy   Then – I dunno what to tell you.

Julie   Well –

– that's fine.

Cos I do.

She starts packing a rucksack.

Romy   Where you going?

Julie   The STAR.

Romy   Alright.

Be quiet coming back in. Cos if she's asleep she won't have been for long.

Julie   See you in a bit.

She kisses him, kisses **Niamh**. *Goes.*

Scene Five

Kath *and* **Col**'s *place.*

Julie *dressed just as she was leaving the last scene.*

Col   Mum said you were looking tired.

Julie   Good of her. She out?

Col   Night shift. How's the baby?

Julie   Still gestating, thanks.

Col   How's it working out at your young / man's place –

Julie   Really great.

Col   Bit cramped, is it.

Julie   We don't mind cramped.

Besides, me and Romy'll be moving out before long.

Col   I thought you couldn't move into the uni flat / till you –

Julie   Seen a place on Broadway, five hundred quid a month.

We can afford that.

Col   Afford it how?

Julie   By working, Dad. I do three days, Romy works three days, we cover each other looking after Niamh. Easy.

Col   Got it all figured out.

Julie   Well, I've had to, haven't I.

Col   Is that how it'll go when you're in uni? Three days a week work, three days a week childcare. Doesn't leave much time for actual studying, does it.

Julie   We'll manage.

Col   How, do you think?

Julie   I didn't know how I'd manage when you chucked me out on the streets but I worked it out, I'll work this out too.

Not so soft as you thought.

Col   Maybe not, no.

It's a genuine admission.

And it means something to her.

Julie   So maybe everything will be alright, Dad.

He doesn't answer.

Col   D'you want something to eat?

Julie   Just ate thanks.

Col   Left over spag bol, you'd be doing me a favour clearing it up.

Julie   Maybe we can swap favours then.

Col   Sure.

Julie   Could I work here for a couple of hours tonight?

Col   Here?

Julie   At the table . . . or in my room. Wherever.

Col   I see.

Julie   It's just cos Nevey's teething. Just this once.

Col   Do you know how long teething lasts?

Julie   It doesn't matter because I won't ask again cos I'll sort something else out. But tonight, this once, can I work here please.

Col   Why are you still working?

Julie   Cos I've got A levels?

Col   You only need two Cs.

Julie   And?

Col   You could get two Cs without even trying.

Julie   But I am trying, to make sure I definitely do.

Col   You still wanna get the grades for Cambridge.

Julie   Not really.

Col   I know you, girl.

Julie   Do you.

Col   I've known you all your life.

Julie   At my interview they let us have this room with water and biscuits to wait in and I got talking to this girl, posh but nice enough, and we're having nice chats and getting on and she says to me –

– did you go to a good school?

And I thought about it and I thought Bro Edern bit shit but enough of the teachers really try, you know? And I say – yeah. Yeah I do go to a good school.

And she says – oh. Which one? And I'm like – *which one?*

Like she's heard of all the decent schools in Britain?

And I say, oh Bro Edern. She's blank. I say it's a Welsh medium comp in Cardiff.

And she freezes, doesn't say another word. And Miss Evans asked how it'd gone and I told her about this girl. She said, to posh people, 'a good school' means specific schools. The oldest, most expensive public schools there are. Eton, Harrow, few others. There's like half a dozen of them. So when I said yes I went to a good school, that's what she thought I meant. And when I said I went to a comprehensive – she freaked out. She literally could not say another word to me. Because I went to a comprehensive.

Like fucking basically everybody in the world does. And Cambridge is all people like that.

And you think I should go there? And become like them?

Col   Then why are you still trying to?

Julie   Cos I wanna know I could. I wanna know I'm as good as them.

Col   You're not as good as them.

You're better. Cos everything you've done, you didn't have half the help these posh kids had. You had what we could manage.

Julie   Then help me prove it. Let me work here tonight. Just for a couple of hours.

I won't tell Mum I promise. Dad, please.

Col   You made your choice, love. Now live it.

Scene Six

Barb's *place. The place is dark. The settee folded out into a bed. The Moses basket next to the settee.*

Romy *comes awake.*

Sits up a bit, bleary. Then lies back down.

Then something strikes him. He looks in the Moses basket.

She's not there. And then **Julie**'s *voice.*

Julie   And then the middle of the galaxy, there's this massive black hole.

Julie's *in a corner, with cushions and pillows and blankets made into a kind of nest. She's got* **Niamh**, *snoozing in her arms. A quantum physics book open on her lap.* **Romy** *settles back down, acts like he's still asleep.*

Julie   And we can't see it. But we know it must be there, because it's what holds the galaxy together. Everything would go flying off into space without it.

She pauses.

Julie   I know you're awake.

Romy   I'm not.

Julie   You've stopped snoring.

Romy   I love listening to you read to her.

Julie   Calms me down.

Romy   Calms her down as well. What d'you need calming from?

Julie   Bring me the basket?

He does. **Julie** *carefully – expertly – lays sleeping* **Niamh** *down in the Moses basket.*

Romy   How was the library?

Julie   Oh you know. Full of nutters.

Romy   Bet you fit right in.

Julie   I fed you that line.

Romy   Get everything you needed done?

Julie   Yeah, you know.

Romy   Next time she wakes, it's my turn.

Julie   So not arguing.

Romy   Coming to bed settee?

Julie   Yeah I'll be in bed settee in five minutes.

Romy   I'm really fucking horny. Like ridiculous.

Julie   People say to me sometimes, what is it you see in that Romeo Jones and I tell them –

– when he speaks it's like poetry falls from his lips.

Romy   . . . and it gets you foaming at the fanny.

Julie   Gushing at the gash.

Romy   I hate gash, that's vile.

Julie   You love mine, you dirty bitch.

Romy   Now I'm grossed out and turned on at the same time.

Julie   And now you know how a straight woman feels when she sees a pair of balls.

Romy   If you're not in the mood for a very, very quiet whatever then I'm gonna nip to the bathroom and knock one out otherwise I'm gonna be tossing and turning all night keeping us both up –

Julie   Much better you toss in the bathroom.

Romy   Well, that's what I thought.

And then something changes in **Julie**.

Romy *sees it.*

Romy   What?

Julie   Nothing. Off you trot, have your toss.

Romy   I think I've just lost the will to wank.

They look at each other.

Romy   Can you tell me something?

Julie   Like what?

Romy   Something amazing. Like you were telling her about the black hole at the centre of the galaxy.

She doesn't answer.

Romy   Just one of those amazing things whirling round your head.

Julie   Bit too shattered to be amazing now.

Romy   Yeah, course.

Me too.

Julie *flops down, pulls the covers around her.*

Julie   Climb in. Let's be shattered together.

Romy *stands for a moment –*

– then settles beside her.

They sleep, time passes.

And then **Romy** *gets up.*

Looks down at **Julie**.

Then he puts on a BabyBjörn, or similar. Lowers **Niamh** *into it.*

Goes.

Scene Seven

The playground. **Romy**'*s on the bench, the buggy near him.*

Julie *approaches. They kiss each other hello.* **Julie** *leans over the buggy, saying hello to* **Niamh**.

Romy   So. I been wondering something. About Stormzy.

This is somewhat from left field.

Julie   Is that Stormzy my cousin Hannah's corn snake, or Stormzy the grime artist.

Romy   The rapper.

Julie   Yeah cos what do you care about snakes?

Romy   You know Stormzy pays for kids to go to university.

Why does he pay for kids to go to Cambridge, not Cardiff?

Julie   Right.

Romy   If they're both as good as each other.

Julie   Stormzy hates Cardiff. He's got massive beef with Benjy from Astroid Boys.

Romy   Did he link with Benjy's girl at the coffee shop?

Julie   Worse than that, Benjy scoffed Stormzy's panini backstage at Tramshed. And you know what Stormzy's like about his paninis.

A moment.

Romy   I went to the university.

Julie   You did what?

Romy   I went – like, I walked up by the museum, asked some kid where the university was. And then I talked to this bloke. This lecturer. And he told me, Cardiff isn't as good as Cambridge.

Julie   He actually said that to you?

Romy   At first he bullshitted for a bit about how it was very old-fashioned to think Oxbridge was necessarily the best. And then I said you'd got a place but then I'd got you pregnant and now you weren't gonna go. And then –

He said it's all about money. In Cambridge they can afford the tutors to have you write an essay every week. And then the tutor sits with you for an hour and tells you in detail why it's shit.

But Cardiff you maybe do one actual essay a term. So you would learn eight times less in Cardiff.

Julie   Do you have any idea how useless my physics teacher is in school? Lovely bloke, his hair oh my God you wanna plunge your hands into it – but not a clue. He actually asks me for help, explaining the hard stuff?

Romy   We're not talking about school.

Julie   What I learn has got sod all to do with how much they teach. What I learn is down to me and how much I push myself.

Romy   And how will that work when you've got a baby?

Julie   I'm gonna dump the baby on you.

Romy *just looks at her.*

Julie   Well, I won't be able to piss about obviously.

Romy   You're taking a year off, before you even go to uni.

Julie   Because I'm being realistic about –

Romy   And then when your baby's really little, you'll go off to study.

Julie   People do.

Romy   And become the best in the world?

Cos I don't mean to be a dick but you look fuckin shattered now –

She can't.

Julie   Romy, of course Cambridge is better than Cardiff for doing a degree. Of course it is.

Romy   Then why d'you say it wasn't?

Julie   Because –

– it doesn't matter.

Romy   How can you lying to me not matter?

Julie   I didn't want you to feel guilty.

Romy   About fucking up your life?

Julie   See – this is why, this now.

Romy   Every time you've said yeah it's fine they're basically the same – you were lying.

Julie   I thought you knew.

Romy   No you didn't.

Julie   Yeah, I did.

Romy   How would I know something like that?

Julie   You know Cambridge asked me for A star, A star, A. And Cardiff offered me two Cs. Why would it be so hard for me to get in to Cambridge and loads easier to get in to Cardiff, if they were the same?

Cos you're not fuckin thick are you. You knew.

Romy   I knew you were giving up all your dreams you've had since you were twelve?

Julie   Yes. And it's fine.

Romy   It fuckin is not.

Julie   Romy: what are the chances I was really going to be the next Stephen Hawking? Julie from Splott is gonna discover the theory of everything? I love that you really believe I could but –

Romy   Course you could.

Julie   Technically *anyone* could.

Romy   You used to believe you could.

Julie   It was something I used to say cos I thought it sounded cool.

Romy   It didn't sound cool. It sounded like the spoddiest thing anyone's ever said in their lives.

But you used to believe it. You used to think you had a chance.

Julie   Or I've got a chance to be loved. And to love. And to have a family.

And I still get to learn about gamma ray bursts and black holes.

That's more than most people even dare dream of.

Romy   Just you don't get to change the world.

Julie   What does that even mean?

It feels like you've changed my world.
Like I never thought I would be a mum, or
Look after a baby, and now I know I can / and –

Romy   So basically I got you up the duff . . .

She grabs a board book from the basket under the pram. Opens it, shoves it into his hands.

Julie   Read that.

Romy   I can't.

Julie   Don't be pathetic. Fucking try.

He tries.

Romy   The . . . strong for –
   The strong force holds the –

He shows her a word.

Romy   No idea.

Julie   Nucleus.

Romy   The strong force holds the nucleus together.

Julie   See it feels like I changed your world too.
   Fuckin tell me that's not worth doing. I dare you.

They look at each other.

Julie   Romy.

Romy   Christ I feel sick now.

Julie   Then just sit tight and shut up for a bit.

Romy   I don't know what I'm doing. And if I was stuck with anything else the person I'd ask would be you.

Julie   And you'd be very sensible to do that, because I'm very clever, I keep up to date on all the latest thinking, and I've got your best interests at heart.

And I can see you're getting all panicky and worried what / you should –

Romy   I just think that if everything was fine you wouldn't have been fuckin lying to me.

Julie   I think first – calm the fuck down.

I think second – okay yeah with the whole Cambridge v. Cardiff thing I got it wrong. I thought it was one of those things we understood between us without needing to put it into words.

Romy   We haven't got any things like that.

Julie   We've got loads of things like that.

Romy   We have but they're all about sex.

And they're together again.

Julie   You've gotta listen to me now, okay.

If I tell you I don't want to go away, I don't want to leave, then you have to listen to that.

I know what is best for me.

Romy   And staying here with me is best for you.

Julie   That's what I want.

She didn't quite answer the question.

He's looking at her.

She moves closer to him.

Touches him somehow.

He allows it, needs it, can't bear it.

Julie   It's okay. See? It's okay.

Romy   How can it be okay?

Julie   Because we –

– we found each other.

We got so lucky.

Romy *hugs her. And* **Julie***'s hoping it's the end of the matter but for* **Romy** *it's a leave-taking. And in the end he breaks it.*

Romy   Do you know what I think?

She shakes her head.

Romy   I think, is it

You really want to have a baby, right now

Or is it,

You can't bear to get rid of a baby we made.

Julie   I want a baby with you right now.

She answered too quick and she knows it.

How would I even know the difference, between how those two things feel?

Romy   It's obvious.

Julie   Not to me, and I'm the brainy one.

Romy   If we weren't together, would you still have it?

Or would you get rid of it, and go off to Cambridge?

Julie   Having a baby by yourself is a different thing.

Romy   Oh I know.

Julie   Okay then – now you put it that way,

Yes. Yes if we weren't together,

I would still have this baby, rather than going off to Cambridge.

Satisfied?

Romy   Then have her.

She's not sure what he's saying.

Romy   Have her without me.

Julie   You're – you're finishing with me?

Romy   You want a baby,

Have her on your own, like I did.

Julie   D'you think you're doing this for me?

D'you think you're doing this to save me?

You're not. I love you, and I love Nevey, and I'll love our baby. That's not a mistake.

You're making the mistake.

You're ruining everything, right now, for nothing. Romy.

He's getting himself together to go.

You fucking idiot.

He's really going.

Alright alright alright just tell me one thing.

He stops.

> In your guts –
> In your heart,
> Leaving me
> Does that feel like the right thing?

Romy   Yes it does.

Julie   I could walk over there right now
Put my hand on your cheek and you
Would be in pieces. You know it.

She's moving towards him.

Romy   Don't.

Don't you fuckin dare.

She lets his anger land. Lets it hurt her. Lets him see. He's aching to go to her.

Julie   Romy. Please.

He goes.

Scene Eight

Kath and **Col**'s *place.*

Kath and **Julie** *sat near one another.*

Kath   The thing is,
We're all stupid sometimes.
Look at your dad.

Julie   What about him?

Kath   Nothing in particular, just look at him. Stupid, isn't he?

Julie   You think you could've done better?

Kath   I still might.

They sit.

Julie   This is the right thing to do. Stopping it.

Kath   It's up to you, love.

Julie   I know you think it is, so just say it is.

Kath   Of course it bloody is. You can have a kid whenever. You don't need one now.

Julie   I won't miss feeling shattered all the time.

But I sort of will.

Kath   You'll miss it for a bit. And then – you'll have so much else going on.

Julie   And I won't regret it?

Kath   No. Course you won't.

Julie   Mum.

Kath   You'll feel sad sometimes. You will.
You'll never think you made the wrong choice, deciding to have a life for yourself.

Julie   D'you feel sad sometimes . . . that you took me on.

Kath   What d'you mean?

Julie   I mean – you didn't have to. You could've just – had a life for yourself. But you took me on when I was tiny and you looked after me and you –

– you chose to be my mum.

Kath   This is not – we are not / talking about –

Julie   D'you ever wish you hadn't.

Kath *almost can't answer.*

Kath   Being your mum is the best I thing I've ever done. Don't you dare –

Julie   So why isn't being a mum the best thing I could do? Why's it different?

Kath   You know
My clients. Most of them
I do twenty minutes, twice a day.
Get them up, put them to bed.
A couple I'm in there afternoons too but –

Some of them,
I'm not just the person that gets them up
The person that feeds them

The person that washes them –
Some of them,
I'm the only person they speak to.
The only person that ever touches them.
I'm the only person they see.
You talk to them,
I'm their bloody angel.
But –

The warmth fades from her.

The time the agency pay me,
That twenty minutes,
It's not enough. It's not enough
To be a person's whole life.

Course it's not.
So then it's, do I do more,
Because they need more from me?
Or do I leave them?
Some of them are dying, it's their last days and
I'm supposed to leave them, twenty minutes on the dot
Cause that's what I'm paid for?
Not a chance.
I give them, whatever they need.
I make sure they feel, like they matter.
And where does that come from, that extra?
It comes from me.
It comes from me, and
Every day I've got a bit less left
For you, for your dad.
For myself.
And the bloke that owns the agency
He gets richer every day, because he knows
What I do will always be more than what he pays me.
And that's the best part of me
The part that means I
Can't leave those poor sods,
And just walk away.

And that man, that millionaire
A dozen times over
Takes the piss out of the best part of me
Every single day.

That is not gonna be you.
Whatever you do, you're not gonna be
Where I am, where your dad is, where everyone
On this street is.

Julie   So I leave you and Dad and Romy and Niamh and everyone, everyone has to live like that, But I get away? And that's good enough, is it?

Kath   Of course it's not good enough, love.

It's the best I can manage.

They sit.

Julie   I'm really scared of doing it. Going through it.

Kath   I know.

I will not leave you, for a second.

Her love is too much for **Julie** *to cope with.*

Julie   I'm so sorry.

Kath   It's okay. It's okay.

Eventually **Julie** *collects herself.*

Kath   So we know what we're doing.

Julie   Yeah.

Kath   Good.

It's the right thing.

It is.

Julie *nods.*

Kath   It's awful, isn't it.
       Actually being in charge of your life.

       You know the only thing that's worse?
       Not being.

Scene Nine

The playground.

Romy *cuddling* **Niamh**, *feeding stuff over the bench.*

From off –

Col   Oi!

He enters quickly.

You little shit.

Romy Would you mind your language please.

Col I'll use whatever fucking language I / like, mate –

Romy Would you mind your language in front of my baby please.

Col *gets hold of himself.*

Col Your baby's screwed anyway, mate, with a shit like you for a dad.

Romy*'s settling* **Niamh** *in the buggy, making to leave.*

Romy This man's being a bit silly isn't he, Nevey.

Col D'you know what my daughter's doing this afternoon?

Getting your baby fucking scraped out of her.

This brings **Romy** *to a halt.*

He recovers, gets on with packing up to go.

Romy Okay.

Col That all you got to say?

Romy She got somebody with her?

Col Of course she bloody has.

Romy Good.

Col Good?

Romy Good she's got somebody.

Col Makes you feel less guilty does it?

Romy Alright, Nevey, we'll be going now.

Col One day I'm gonna run in to you. And you won't have that kid to hide behind.

Romy *stops, looks at him.*

Romy Fair enough, mate.

Col   Yeah I'm looking forward to it.

Romy   You know I love her.

Col   You don't know the meaning of the word.

Romy   She's the best thing that ever happened to me.
After Nevey.

Col   I bet she fucking is. And you knocked her up and ran.

Romy   Fuckin look at me, mate. I'm not the running type.

Col   But that's what you did.

Romy   So what –

– shall I phone her?

Shall I phone her now and tell her I made a horrible mistake
and I'm sorry?

Col   She'd tell you to fuck off.

Romy   Shall I tell her I want her to have the baby?

Col   Do what you like.

Romy   Okay then.

He reaches for his phone.

Col   Don't you dare.

Romy   Why not?

Col   You've messed her around enough.

Romy   I'm not messing around now, mate, I mean it.

Col   I will rip that fucking phone out of / your hands –

Romy   I thought you were pissed off I finished with her? So
I'll take her back. Isn't that what you want?

Col   You better fucking not.

A little pause.

Romy   Why not?

If I've broken her heart, why don't I just unbreak it.

Col   Because she's better off without you.

The truth.

Romy   I know.

I know.

He slumps down onto the bench.

Col *stands there, watches him.*

This broken boy.

And then **Col** *steps towards him.*

Places a hand on his shoulder.

Romy *doesn't flinch, but just freezes.*

And then the freeze is gone.

It's just a tiny moment.

And then **Col** *goes.*

Scene Ten

Kath *and* **Col**'s *place.*

Julie *comes in, dressed a little smarter than you might expect for travel.*

She stops, checks through things in a little day bag.

Col *comes in, hulking a rucksack and a big suitcase.*

Col   We're gonna need to stop off, check the air in the tyres.

Kath *enters, also carrying bags. She dumps them.*

Julie   I could've just got the train.

Col   My little girl goes to Cambridge University, I'm driving her there.

Just to make sure you actually go.

He takes a bag out to the car.

Kath   You set?

Julie   Yeah.

Kath   Been for a wee?

Julie   Yeah, you?

Kath   Oh ha ha.

Julie   Woman your age. All it takes is Dad to say something funny on the drive . . .

Kath   I think we're safe there then aren't we.

Col *comes back for more bags.*

Kath   I did notice that model volcano you had to make in year 5, still in your room?

Julie   Just send it once I'm settled in?

Kath   Fair enough.

Col *comes for the last bag.*

Kath   That's us then.

Julie *gets ready to go.*

But can't quite.

Kath   Nerves?

Julie   Maybe.

Kath   Bound to be.

Julie *can't quite bring herself.*

Kath   What?

Julie   D'you think, if me and Romy had met, say ten years' time –

Kath   What would you be doing back here in ten years?

Julie   Having you put in a nursing home?

Julie *waits but* **Kath** *doesn't give an answer.*

Julie   Mum.

Kath   I think

Ten years from now, God knows what you're going to be. But you're gonna be something amazing.

And Romy's gonna be the same kid pushing a pram round Splott. Nice enough. But nothing more.

And then **Col** *comes in.*

Col   We fit?

Kath   Let's say we are. Or we never / will be.

Julie   Can I run and see him?

Kath   Absolutely no.

Julie   Five minutes. Two minutes. One. Just to say goodbye.

Kath'*s about to shut her down.*

Col   Go on. Five minutes.

She goes.

Kath   What if she doesn't come back?

Col   Then – we have got a lot of things wrong.

Scene Eleven

Barb'*s flat.*

Julie *has literally run.*

Julie   Cos yes, you were right.
  It was the right thing for me to go away
  And do my degree but –
  What if we just try?
  Because – think about it – the terms are only eight weeks.
  Three eights is twenty-four there's fifty-two weeks a year
  I'm here, twenty-eight weeks. I'm here,
  More than I'm there.

Romy   No I get it.

Julie   Then why not?

Romy   You're at some party. Talking about some quantum mechanics shit to some posh boy.

Julie   And that boy won't be you, / so why –

Romy   No he won't be me cos he'll actually understand what you're on about.

You're gonna have a nice time talking to him.

And you're not gonna want to stop talking to him.

Julie   But I'll be coming back to you.

Romy   You'll come back to me. Because you have to. Because you promised you would.

Julie   No, because I'll want to!

Romy   And it'll be there in your eyes, that you wish you didn't have to come back to me.

And seeing that will fucking ruin me.

Julie   That's not gonna happen.

Romy   You promise, that's not gonna happen?

She can't.

Julie   Aren't I worth the risk?

Romy   Course you are.

Julie   I am?

Romy   Course you fuckin are.

Julie   So then we can try –

Romy   You know you said
You never missed your mum. Your birth mum.
You were so young that you don't remember her
So it's like you never lost her.

But you did lose her.
You just don't remember it.
You'll've cried for her.
And held out your arms for her.
And woke in the night
Not knowing where she was
And there was nothing your dad could do
But cuddle you till you cried yourself
Back to sleep.

And when you go away
It's not just me you're leaving.
You're leaving Nevey.
Cos she loves you now.
When you go,
She'll cry for you.
You'll come back Christmas, and
She'll get used to loving you again
Then you'll go. Again.
She'll cry for you. Again.
And you'll do that to her, for years?
Letting her love you
Then leaving her to cry herself to sleep
Over and over, for years
Till one day
You don't come back at all.

Can you do that to her?

Julie *can't answer. Shakes her head.*

Romy Cos you love her, don't you.

She does.

Julie So what then? I just go? That's just it?

He can't say it.

Julie No. No it's not.
   I'll go, I'll do my degree and
   When it's done, I'm coming back. For good.

Romy Okay.

Julie I fuckin am.

Romy I know.

Julie You don't believe me.

Romy I do.

Julie You don't. You don't.
   And you have to.

   You have to believe I'm coming back
   Or I can't leave you.

He knows what he has to do.

Romy We'll go up the mountain
   Stars everywhere we look
   The Milky Way stretching across the sky
   And you'll tell us amazing things about black holes
   And where the universe comes from.
   You, and me, and Nevey and
   Our family.
   I believe it.

It's enough.

Romy Do you want to give her a *cwtsh* goodbye?

Julie Yeah course I –

Julie *steps forwards to takes* **Niamh**. *And then stops.*

Romy *sees her realise.*

Julie   If I take her now –

– if I feel her start to wake and fuss I'll never –

He knows.

Settles **Niamh** *back into his neck.*

Julie   What do I do? What do I do?

Romy   You go.
And be brilliant
For all of us.

The End.

9 781350 408944